The National Debt Crisis: America's Armageddon

—⚇—

Why a Default on US Treasuries

May Be the Only Viable Solution

Morris V Franco

ISBN: 1495326772
ISBN 13: 9781495326776

Dedication

To the Franco family for a lifetime of closeness:
Victor and Rachel
David and Doris
Annette, Dorothy, and Rosalie

To my friends for their support and encouragement in writing this book:
David Shargel
Al Goldstein
Bernie Castor
Richard Jankowitz

Contents

Preface

In the annals of American history, there are few internal threats more ignored or misunderstood than the national debt. The ignorance of the general public on this issue is the result of a deliberate and highly successful strategy of our political leadership. The purpose for this out-of-sight, out-of-mind political agenda is to limit the anxiety Americans would surely feel if they understood the real damage an out-of-control national debt inflicts on our economy and citizens. In this book, I will show you how this happens. I tackle this issue from many angles in order to give the reader the best-possible understanding of the issue of national debt.

I will make clear that the interest burden on taxpayers for funding the national debt is a larger problem than the size of the national debt itself. I will prove that within three to five years after the Federal Reserve starts to normalize interest rates, annual debt interest will exceed the $1 trillion mark and 20–25 percent of every tax dollar collected will go toward funding the debt. I will show you why the government has boxed itself into a situation that makes it nearly impossible to pay down the debt; in fact, in a normal interest-rate environment, it will be next to impossible just to balance the budget.

The national debt is a problem that all by itself could bring the end to America as we know it. It could literally threaten the capitalist form of government that has kept us prosperous and allowed us to defend the freedoms that the Constitution grants to every citizen. The national debt is a disease that first infected the government during the Reagan era, grew steadily through the two Bush presidencies, and reached epidemic proportions under the Obama administration. Curing this disease will require a superhuman effort by our leadership. We are close to the point of no return, in which there will be no way to resolve the problem, meaning that the United States will have to restructure its debt and default on a portion of it. The national debt is a sickness on the verge of becoming terminal!

When I try to explain the importance of this issue, all too often the response is indifference. In my opinion, it is probable that if the general public had understood the scope of the problem and the contribution that the president and Congress make to it, the results of the 2012 election would have been much different.

There are six chapters in this book. All are independent of one another, and each looks at the issue from a different perspective. The more I looked at this issue, the more I became convinced that there was more to be said. There was about a six-month lag between my writing of chapters 3 and 4, because that is how long it took me to realize that a partial default on the national debt by the US government was a real possibility. The first version of the book was published in July 2014. Chapters 5 and 6 are additions to the first edition and were written at least one year after the original publication. The numbers and dates used throughout this book were based on the most current information available at the time.

As I see it, our political leadership by President Obama is taking the country in the wrong direction. For more than a decade, self-responsibility has been on the decline while government dependency has been steadily increasing. On issue after issue, government policies do more harm than good. Citizens who receive government checks just want to see them keep coming and care little about other issues. Municipal and government pensions are outrageously generous. Teachers, police officers, firefighters, sanitation workers, and other unionized civil-service workers donate generously to politicians, who, in turn, use the money to support these laborers' lucrative pay and pension benefits.

Medical benefits, welfare benefits, food stamp benefits, unemployment benefits—there seems to be no limit to the amount of benefits the government is willing to provide. It's nice to be generous, but you can't spend money you don't have. Politicians act as if the national debt is a limitless source of funds. They give the impression that they view the budget overruns that created the national debt as loans that never have to be repaid. There is little concern about the need for a balanced budget or that it will cost taxpayers hundreds of billions of dollars just to cover the interest on the national debt that is being incurred, and it is only getting worse every year.

Notes on Second Edition

In the first edition of this book, I predicted that overall interest rates would be somewhere between 4 and 6 percent by 2017. I made the calculation sometime in 2012 or 2013. At the time, the Federal Reserve's low (near-zero) interest rate policy had been in effect for three or four years. The Fed, as well as just about every other economist, was predicting that the normalization of interest rates would take place in six-to-twelve months. Therefore predicting an increase in interest rates from the average of 1 or 2 percent to a more normal 4 or 5 percent by 2017 was a no-brainer. However things did not work out that way. The prediction that the Federal Reserve would return to more normal rates was based on the assumption that the economy was about to start growing at a strong pace. Instead, the economy remained sluggish, and, to this day, it has been averaging less-to-2 percent annual growth. This forced the Federal Reserve to keep delaying its start date for normalizing rates. As I am writing this in September 2015, the Fed is expected to move up rates at a slower-than-usual pace beginning in late 2015 or early 2016. If this is the case, then my prediction of an average 5 percent interest rate is not likely to happen before 2019 or 2020. Therefore, my earlier prediction of the time when $1 trillion debt interest payments would begin also has to be pushed back to 2019 or 2020.

Chapter 1: Overview

The United States is a superpower and a democracy that thrives on capitalism. We may not be the only superpower, but we are by far the strongest economic and military power on earth. Our economy (GDP) is almost double the size of China's, whose population is four times the size of ours; triple the size of Japan's; and eight times the size of Russia—countries that are second, third, and ninth, respectively, on the world economic scale.

The United States became an economic power in the late 1800s through the expansion of its industrial base. However, at that time we only needed to maintain a minimal military force because the two oceans that separated us from Europe and Asia gave us added security and our continental neighbors were friendly. Our military presence boomed as a result of the Second World War, culminating in the invention of the atom bomb and, in effect, making us the world's first superpower.

This status guaranteed that countries with other agendas could not threaten our form of government. Actually the only country that could pose a serious threat to us was Russia, which developed an atom bomb shortly after we did and aggressively pushed communism.

We are a democracy and the envy of the free world because of the freedoms we guarantee our citizens; for this reason, we are the enemy of most Communist nations and many theocracies and dictatorships. It would not be right to infer that America has always taken the high road to achieve this status, but that should not lessen the significance of the accomplishments we've achieved in becoming who we are. Most of us Americans take our way of life for granted, with little or no thought about what it took to get here.

There is no rule that says the strongest country on earth should be a democracy, and there is no rule that says a democratically elected government will be a good one. Just look at the many nations that elected hard-line leaders who then turned them into dictatorships.

A strong economy allows a country to build a strong military with minimal hardships on its citizens. However, a strong economy is not a necessity. Russia, for example, was economically a third-world country that built a major military force while its citizens struggled to survive in an anemic economy led by a Communist government. History is full of examples of countries that placed expansionism ahead of the needs of their people.

Imagine a world where the only superpower is not the United States but a theocracy like Iran or a Communist country like Russia under Stalin. Imagine, too, that one of these countries has the military and economic power the United States had achieved by the end of World War II, when we were the only superpower on the planet. Then imagine that our country still has all the laws guaranteeing our freedoms but the economy of a third-world country. After all, it's not impossible. Saudi Arabia is a theocracy with a thriving economy, and democracies with anemic economies litter the world.

In this example, each country has been seeking world domination, and because of its economic power and military strength, it would be capable of making major advances toward achieving its goals.

Thankfully, in actuality the United States is the strongest country on earth both economically and militarily, and we have the resources to defend our way of life. In my opinion there will never be a world where all nations coexist peacefully. I strongly believe that humanity cannot coexist with itself. I laugh at the phrase that often pops up in political speeches: "Especially in these troubled times." In all of recorded history, every time was a troubled time. As I mention elsewhere in this book, right now there are a million religious fanatics who, if they could, would push a button that would kill every man, woman, and child in America.

In order to keep our nation safe, we must remain strong, and we cannot stay strong militarily unless we stay strong economically. Achieving strength is more than just an American issue; it is important to the entire free world. Our allies must have confidence that we will honor our treaties, and our enemies must fear us.

The superpower status we had at the end of World War II has diminished as other nations have played catch-up. However, outside of terrorism there are no external threats. The biggest items in the US budget include defense, health care, education, government pensions, and welfare. The national debt dwarfs all of these in importance. Congressional actions can adjust the other expenses. The interest on the national debt is an expense we must pay, no ifs, ands, or buts. Defaulting on our debt obligations would result in nothing less than a worldwide financial Armageddon.

I believe that by the end of this decade, interest on the national debt will be the biggest expense item the budget. In fact, I estimate that at least 20 percent of every tax dollar collected will go toward paying debt interest. How we got ourselves into this situation would be laughable if it weren't so important. It's very simple: we have a president and a Congress that want a government-dependent society and can't say no to any program that supports that agenda. The increase in the national debt has averaged more than $1 trillion a year during the Obama presidency. Addressing it will require budget cuts and tax increases, but politicians run from this issue. Doing the right thing is not as important as getting reelected. In fact, I believe, most politicians can't grasp or don't care about the problem.

Investors who purchase US Treasury securities that fund the national debt see a country with deteriorating financial stability that will require ever-higher interest rates to buy our debt. Unfortunately our weak-willed politicians have been borrowing from the national debt to pay the interest needed to fund it. How stupid is that? In my opinion, most investors in treasuries are wise to this government scheme, but because the Federal

Reserve purchased more than $4 trillion in securities to keep rates down, there is little chance the interest rates paid on these treasuries will reflect their true credit risk. Once the Fed stops playing hanky-panky with interest rates and lets the free market set the rates, they very likely will spike upward.

The following write-up explains how and why the national debt is out of control and how it has the possibility of harming us and even posing a threat to our democratic form of government.

Making America an Also-Ran

Back in 1917, during the First World War, the government's recruitment effort included the iconic poster featuring Uncle Sam pointing at the viewer accompanied by the phrase "I Want You for US Army." Leaping forward to the year 2012, the same poster would feature Uncle Sam looking viewers in the eye with the phrase "I Want You to Give Me $136,200," as shown in figure 1.1. I wish I were kidding, but unfortunately this is the actual amount the average family (household) owed the US government as its share of the 2013 estimated $16.4 trillion national debt. By June of 2015 the national debt reached $18 trillion, meaning the government borrowed an additional $11,800 from every American household in just the last three years.

Figure 1.1.

The national debt is a looming time bomb that could greatly diminish our standing in the world and cause devastating economic and social damage. When I raise this issue in political discussions, I find the vast majority of people I talk to don't understand what the national debt is. I'll even venture to say that many can't even grasp the term *a trillion dollars.* The size of the debt is staggering, but the interest on the debt that taxpayers will bear is even more staggering and less understood.

When President Obama took office in 2009, the national debt totaled $11.9 trillion. By the time his first term ended, it went up to $16.4 trillion—a 46 percent increase in four years. Half way into his second term, the debt grew to more than $18 trillion. The president claims his deficit spending was less than that of his predecessor, President Bush. This is pure nonsense. Just take a look at the numbers in table 1.1. President Obama accrued a bigger budget deficit in his first four years in office than President Bush did in eight years.

TABLE 1.1. Budget deficits, 2002–2017

Pres.	Year	Deficit	Pres.	Year	Deficit
Bush	2009	$1,412	Obama	2017	$409
Bush	2008	$425	Obama	2016	$474
Bush	2007	$160	Obama	2015	$583
Bush	2006	$248	Obama	2014	$483
Bush	2005	$318	Obama	2013	$680
Bush	2004	$413	Obama	2012	$1,087
Bush	2003	$377	Obama	2011	$1,300
Bush	2002	$157	Obama	2010	$1,293
	Total	$3,510		Total	$6,309

Note: In billions of dollars. Budget deficits for the years 2016 and 2017 are estimates. The InsideGov website (http://www. insidegov.com/) estimates tax revenues in 2017 of $3.32 trillion, expenses (outlays) of $3.72 trillion, a budget deficit of $409 billion, and GDP of $17.4 trillion.

TABLE 1.2. National debt: 2014–2006

Fiscal year	National debt
9/30/2014	$17,824
9/30/2013	$16,738
9/30/2012	$16,066
9/30/2011	$14,790
9/30/2010	$13,561
9/30/2009	$11,909
9/30/2008	$10,024
9/30/2007	$9,007
9/30/2006	$8,506

Note: Figures in billions of dollars. President George W. Bush treated the Iraqi War as an off-budget item. When that $800 billion used to fund that war is added in, it brings the total budget deficit under his administration to $4.31 trillion.

A Wake-Up Call

If I were to pose the question "What are the two largest debt obligations of the average home-owning middle income family?" most Americans would likely say the mortgages on their homes, followed by their car loans or collage loans. Wrong! Wrong! Wrong!

As shown in table 1.3, in 2013, the second-largest debt that the average family owes is their share of the national debt, an outrageous $136,200. They owe this money to the US government because it can't balance its budget. For example, in 2012 President Obama's budget called for $3.8 trillion in spending, but government revenues (mostly taxes) only came to $2.5 trillion. In order to make up for the shortfall, the government had to raise the national debt by borrowing an additional $1.3 trillion.

TABLE 1.3. Average household debt

Average mortgage debt	$199,000
National debt per household	$136,200
Average student loan (per borrower)	$20,835
Average car loan balance	$10,000–$30,000

Note: The 2010 US Census lists the total number of households in this country as 114.8 million, increasing at a rate of about 1.3 million a year. Extending this out two years to 2012 brings the number of households to 117.4 million. Dividing the 2012 total deficit of $16.4 trillion by this number equates to $136,200 of debt per household. According to a July 2012 posting on the MSNBC website, the average mortgage loan balance was near $200,000, and the median home price was just over $170,000, meaning the average home was valued at 15 percent below the loan balance because of the bursting of the housing bubble.

The Obama National Debt Bomb and the Sad Truth

Please excuse this little fish story. When President Obama took office on January 20, 2009, the first bill he signed with the blessing of Congress was the "Credit Card for Every Household" bill, giving every household a credit card and the opportunity to borrow up to $42,000 from lending institutions of their choice. This was quickly followed up by a second bill called the "Bail Out America" bill, requiring every household to use up its newly received credit line—to borrow the entire $42,000 and give it as a gift to the US government to help it balance its budget and pay its bills. In addition, each borrower was still responsible for repaying the $42,000 to the lending institution.

Then, by executive order, the president decreed that borrowers could indefinitely delay repayment of the loans' principals as long as they paid the interest on the loans. The good deeds never end. Then, also by executive order, he allowed the borrowers to charge the interest on their loans to their credit card. Wow! What a great president. He allowed us to give the government $42,000 plus interest without ever taking a dime out of our own pockets. Then we reelected President Obama to reward him for his economic expertise. After all, who else could spend $5.1 trillion and charge it all?

Obviously, the names of the bills and the executive orders are fictitious, but it is true that during President Obama's first term, the federal government forced every household to lend it $42,000. The national debt under President Obama increased at more than double the rate than it did under President Bush. (Note: The $42,000 figure comes from the actual and projected deficits for the years 2010 to 2013, totaling $5.1 trillion, divided by the total household figure of $117.4 million. It comes to $42,666, to be exact.)

Creating awareness of the national debt issue in the general public is a daunting task. The issue is complex, and the numbers are staggering. Nevertheless it is crucial to make the voting public aware of the issue. Ignorance of it greatly helps the party in power, which is especially clear when you consider the massive increases in the national debt during President Obama's first term and the history of Congress playing fast and loose with taxpayer dollars. Only the media can create public awareness of this issue. However, outside of a few financial networks and business magazines, this issue receives very little attention.

The only way to pay down the national debt is through a budget surplus, and given the size of the budget deficits in recent years, we can forget about one happening any time soon. Just remember that 40 percent of the 2012 budget was devoted to deficit spending. Can you imagine the congressional uproar if it had to close a 40 percent budget gap through tax increases and spending cuts? The Democratic leadership is adamant about not cutting entitlement programs, and the Republican leadership is equally adamant about not raising taxes. So the best we can hope for is a reduction in the amount the deficit will increase. The Office of Management and Budget forecasts the budget will be at $4.5 trillion in 2017, with a deficit $612 billion. The total national debt is expected to reach $20 trillion that year.

Interest on the National Debt

Most of the national debt is in the form of US government securities, yielding various interest rates. The government makes interest and principal payments to the holders of the securities. It is one of the major expenses included in the annual budget. The interest on the debt averaged about $350 billion annually early during the Bush presidency, reaching $450 billion in his final year in office. The amount of interest paid during the Obama presidency has been substantially lower due to record-low interest rates the Federal Reserve set to help revive the economy from the 2007–'08 recession. I will fully explain the effect of Federal Reserve interest rate policies on the national debt later in this book.

Interest rates are determined by supply and demand. When demand exceeds supply, it pushes interest rates down because the government can sell securities at a lower rate. An example of this was the demand for US securities by European investors, who viewed them as a safe alternative during the European financial crisis. Conversely, when supply exceeds demand, the government is forced to increase the interest rate in order to spur demand.

Budget deficits, which are the borrowings that make up the national debt, are turned into actual cash by the Federal Reserve through the issuance of Treasury bills, notes, and bonds backed by the full faith and credit of the US government. When you hear the phrase "The Fed is printing money," this is what it means.

The purchaser of these securities will receive interest payments from the government, as shown in table 1.4. In general, the longer the term of the security, the higher the interest rate. Treasury bills are issued for one year or less, and the interest is earned by reducing the purchase price without reducing the maturity value. Treasury notes are issued with maturities of up to ten years, and Treasury bonds have maturities of up to thirty years. In both cases, interest payments are made every six months.

TABLE 1.4. Interest paid on the national debt by the
by the US government, 2007–2017

Year	Debt interest paid	Year	Debt interest paid
2007	$429	2013	$415
2008	$451	2014	$430
2009	$383	2015	$390
2010	$413	2016	$482
2011	$454	2017	$565
2012	$359		

Note: Figures in billions of dollars. Interest statistics retrieved
from the TreasuryDirect website (www.treasurydirect.gov). The
figures for the years 2015 through 2017 are the government's
own estimates.

Future National Debt Payments

The government estimates that when and if the national debt reaches
$20 trillion in 2017, the interest on it will be about $565 billion. This
equates to an average interest rate on the entire debt of just 2.83 percent. In my opinion, this is a gross underestimate. Look at the following
list in table 1.5 covering 1988 through 2015. The average rate over the
twenty-four-year period was just above 4 percent. Applying that rate to
a $20 trillion national debt equates to an annual debt interest payment of
$800 billion. If I were to average in the Paul Volcker years (August 1979
to August 1987), which included high inflation and record-high interest
rates, the average interest rate would be well north of 5 percent and would
require debt interest well in excess of $1 trillion.

TABLE 1.5. National debt statistics, 1988–2015

President	Year	Debt interest	Total national in billions	Average debt in billions
Obama	2015	251	$18,200	1.38%
Obama	2014	430	$17,824	2.41%
Obama	2013	415	$16,788	2.47%
Obama	2012	359	$16,066	2.23%
Obama	2011	454	$15,125	3.00%
Obama	2010	413	$14,024	2.94%
Obama	2009	383	$12,311	3.11%
Bush	2008	451	$10,699	4.22%
Bush	2007	429	$9,229	4.65%
Bush	2006	405	$8,680	4.67%
Bush	2005	352	$8,170	4.31%
Bush	2004	321	$7,596	4.23%
Bush	2003	318	$7,001	4.54%
Bush	2002	332	$6,405	5.18%
Bush	2001	359	$5,943	6.04%
Clinton	2000	361	$5,662	6.38%
Clinton	1999	353	$5,776	6.11%
Clinton	1998	363	$5,614	6.47%
Clinton	1997	355	$5,502	6.45%
Clinton	1996	343	$5,323	6.44%
Clinton	1995	332	$4,988	6.66%
Clinton	1994	296	$4,800	6.17%
Clinton	1993	292	$4,535	6.44%
Bush	1992	292	$4,177	6.99%
Bush	1991	286	$3,801	7.52%
Bush	1990	264	$3,364	7.85%
Bush	1989	240	$2,952	8.13%
Reagan	1988	214	$2,684	7.97%
28-year average		9663	$233,239	4.14%
20-year average '88–'07		6507	$112,202	5.80%

TABLE 1.6. Sample budget items, actual and estimated

	2014	Estimated by CBO for 2017
Pensions	$915	$1,070
Health care	$921	$1,160
Defense	$799	$800
Interest	$229	$391
Federal deficit	–$484	–$457
My estimate of debt interest		$1,000
National debt	$17,824	$20,261

Note: Figures in billions of dollars.
Source: US Government Spending website (http://www. usgovernmentspending.com); 2017 estimates by the CBO.

As you can see, debt interest payment in excess of $1 trillion exceeds anything in the 2015 budget and would be among the largest expenses in the 2017 budget. Is the 5 percent estimated rate reasonable? If history is any indicator, it sure is, but that's not the end of it. There are some dark clouds on the horizon that may affect interest rates. Here are some possibilities:

- The United States loses some of its safe haven status if or when the European and Asian economies stabilize.
- The large and ever-growing debt load discourages investors, who will demand higher interest rates before purchasing US Treasury securities.
- The big three rating agencies (Moody's, S&P, and Fitch) downgrade US debt because of the ever-expanding debt load and seriously unbalanced budgets.
- The Federal Reserve issues a policy change, moving away from the extremely accommodative low-rate policy.

- The liquidation of the $4 trillion in securities bought by the Federal Reserve as part of their "quantitative-easing" program puts pressure on interest rates.
- The government underestimates its budget needs. (The accounting firm Deloitte estimates the cost of health care to be at almost three times its original estimate.)

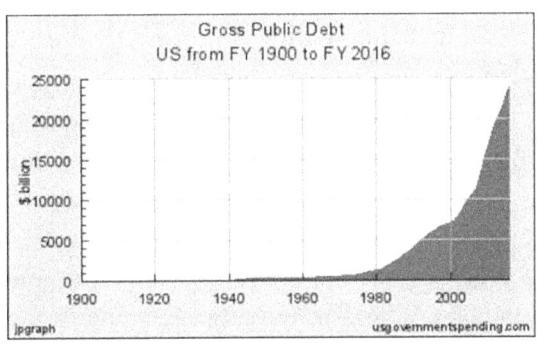

Figure 1.2. US government total debt forecasts.

A Trillion Here, a Trillion There, Pretty Soon You're Talking Real Money! (Thank You, Senator Everett Dirksen)

So if my assumptions are correct, in fewer than five years we will need to use a minimum of $1 trillion of our revenues each year just to pay the interest on our debt—$1 trillion that will bring no, none, zilch, zero benefits to our citizens. That's at least $10 trillion over ten years flushed down the toilet. Since the end of the Second World War, no single budget item other than the deficit has reached that figure—not defense, not welfare, not pensions, and not health care. What benefits have we gotten from our $18 trillion debt? I'm sure there were plenty, but were they worth the price?

Deficit spending should be used only in times of war or other national crises. All other times the budget should be balanced. Just imagine how much better off the country would be today without the debt load. For example, in the five-year period between 2007 and 2011, taxpayers paid

$2.1 trillion just to fund the interest on the debt. That's $410 billion a year that could have been used to better the lives of all Americans.

I wish I could forecast better days ahead, but I can't. I see the debt increasing at a substantial rate for many years. I estimate that the total national debt will easily reach the $20 trillion mark by 2020. I anticipate a diminished United States forced to its knees by the ever-increasing debt load and rising interest rates and required to make drastic cuts to all discretionary programs, including entitlements and the military. I see severe cuts in government programs such as pensions, education, welfare, health care, and student loans. I predict social unrest resulting from these cuts. Problems the government should have addressed years ago will instead be compounded by politicians who want citizens to become dependent on the government without regard of the cost.

President Obama has been looking to raise taxes on individuals with incomes over $250,000. The estimated tax revenue generated from that proposal would range from $60 billion to $80 billion annually. Compare that to the $65 billion in new debt interest we will have to pay as a result of the 2013 budget deficit of $1.3 trillion. The increased debt interest caused by that deficit will almost totally use up the added revenue from taxing the rich. If our leadership had owned up to the increasing debt interest problem, the voting public might have been more resistant to future spending programs out of fear of increased taxes. Our leadership talks so little about the national debt that you'd think the information is classified.

Europe Today; America Tomorrow

The European Union has recently undergone a severe fiscal crisis. Greece's out-of-control spending pushed interest rates so high that the Greek government actually defaulted on its sovereign debt, forcing bond-holders to settle for fewer than fifty cents on a dollar. In order to get help from the European Union, the government had to agree to put its house in order and undertake drastic austerity measures. Unemployment soared, and social unrest became commonplace.

Then Spain and Italy both saw their interest rates rise to unsustainable levels. The Spanish ten-year bond hit 7.5 percent, and Italy's ten-year bond hit 6.5 percent. These rates jeopardized the economies of both countries, and both were looking for and received support from the European Union.

Investors avoid purchasing bonds from countries with out-of-control spending for fear of them defaulting. A country's stability can usually be measured by the interest rates on its sovereign debt. Germany, by far the strongest country in the European Union, has some of the lowest interest rates because investors view its debt as safe. The European Central Bank (ECB), in its effort to stabilize the crises in Spain and Italy, has taken some limited monetary actions with the agreement that these nations enact certain austerity measures. As the ECB's seventeen members fund the institution, anchored by Germany, together they appear to have enough firepower to meet these objectives.

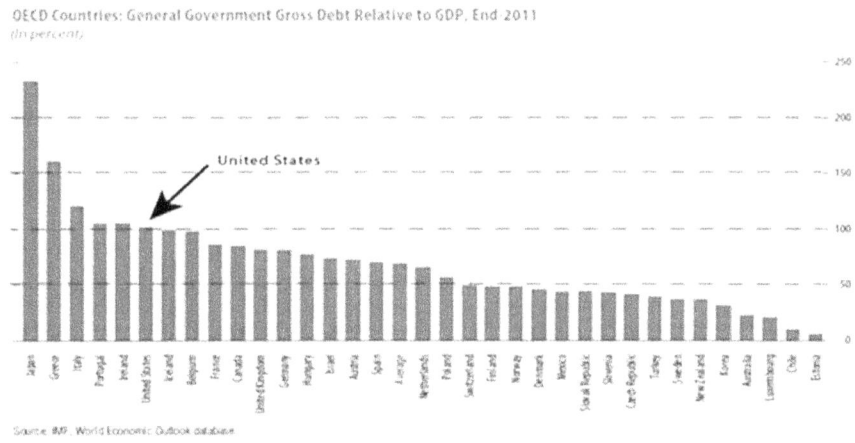

Figure 1.3. Debt-to-GDP ratio by country at the end of 2011.

God Help Us Because Nobody Else Will

Since the end of World War II, the United States has led the world in providing foreign aid. In 1948, we started the Marshall Plan with a $15 billion grant to help Europe recover from the devastation of World War

II. In 2010, US foreign aid reached $52 billion. Why do I write about this? To make the point that no other countries will return our generosity. If America's debt problem creates a fiscal Armageddon, no one will help us out. Our allies will give us verbal support. Our adversaries will be dancing in the streets.

In 2013, the European Union's total sovereign debt was 87.4 percent of its GDP. Germany, the anchor country of the union, came in at a strong 78.4 percent. When President Obama took office in January 2010, the US national debt was around 67 percent of GDP. As of June 2015, the national debt was at $18.3 trillion and our GDP was $17.8 trillion, equating to a debt-to-GDP ratio of just over 102 percent.

Take a look at the following list in table 1.7. The European Union, with its seventeen member countries, had a GDP of nearly $16.6 trillion in 2015. Helping out a country like Greece with a GDP of just over $200 billion seemed like a no-brainer. Recently Italy and Spain were facing financial difficulties. Together, their GDPs were fifteen times that of Greece (about $3.1 trillion). The European Union, along with the International Monetary Fund (IMF), came up with some solutions. Now imagine if the United States, with a GDP of more than $18 trillion, were to get into financial trouble. There is no entity on earth with anywhere near the firepower needed to bail us out.

TABLE 1.7. GDPs of the world's largest countries

Rank	Country	2015 GDP
1	United States	$17,780
2	European Union (17 nations)	$16,584
3	People's Republic of China	$11,212
4	Japan	$4,210
5	Germany	$3,413
6	United Kingdom	$2,853
7	France	$2,470
8	India	$2,308
9	Brazil	$1,904
10	Italy	$1,843
11	Canada	$1,615
10	Korea	$1,435
14	Spain	$1,230
	—	
43	Greece	$207

Note: 2015 GDP in billions of dollars.

Do I think there's a good chance the debt-to-GDP ratio of the United States will remain at more than 100 percent until the end of this decade? I think it's more likely than not. Do I think it's preventable? Yes, but prevention is highly unlikely. The government will address the problem only after it becomes a major fiscal crisis, one that will start with the rating agencies doling out major downgrades.

Our political leadership has little interest in slowing the amount of borrowing needed to meet budget shortfalls and zero interest in achieving a balanced budget. The possibility of producing a budget with a surplus that would reduce the $16 trillion national debt is nonexistent. Eliminating the debt incurred in President Obama's first term would require a payment of about $42,000 by every American household. With the national debt forecasted to reach $20 trillion by 2017, we're talking about a debt load approaching $150,000 per household.

Chapter 2: The Federal Reserve

Devising the government's obligations resulting from our national debt is an evolving process. The two factors that determine how much interest the government must pay are the size of the national debt and the interest rate on the securities issued by the government to finance that debt. The government issues new debt for two reasons:

1. Congress periodically increases the debt ceiling and issues securities as necessary to fund government programs that tax revenues do not fund.
2. Previously issued debt comes due. When the US government pays the holders of securities their principals in full, the securities are retired, and the Federal Reserve must replace them with new securities at current market rates.

The Size of the National Debt

New debt will, of course, always be issued by the government at the prevailing interest rate. Let's say, for example, that the average overall interest rate for our entire national debt held steady at 3 percent for thirty consecutive years. In this scenario, the only thing that would cause the government to pay more annual debt interest would be an increase in the national debt itself. The annual interest on a hypothetical $10 trillion debt at 3 percent would be $300 billion. As the national debt in 2009 was actually $11.9 trillion, the debt interest would have been $57 billion more. The $57 billion is the difference between the hypothetical $10 trillion debt and the actual $11.9 trillion debt.

Three percent is close to the actual average rate at the start of the 2008 recession. Because the Federal Reserve held rates at record lows from 2008 until the present (October 2015), the average interest rate continued to drop throughout the period. By 2014, average interest rate dropped to just 1.3 percent.

Figure 2.1 shows short-term rates (Treasury bill rates) for the ten-and-a-half-year period of 2005 to 2015. This is followed by another graph, in figure 2.2, showing a much longer view—forty-two years, from 1971 to 2013. The year 2008 started with short-term rates at 4.25 percent. By December 16th of that year, the Federal Reserve reduced short-term rates to near zero. This was one of the fastest series of rate reductions in the Fed's history. It is now almost seven years that rates have remained at zero. This is one of the reasons it is understandable that low rates are viewed more as the norm then the exception by the general public. The long-view graph shows that normal rates would on average be in the 5 or 6 percent range.

Figure 2.1. Short view of federally funded short-term interest rates, January 2005–June 2015

Figure 2.2. Long view of federally funded short
term interest rates, 1971–2013

The Effect of Rate Changes on the US Budget

What happens if the economy takes off and the Fed abandons its low interest rate policy and decides to raise the average interest rate from 3 percent to 6 percent? Based on historical data, 6 percent is close to where rates would be in normal economic times.

In the example in table 2.3, I assume that the Fed just raised the average interest rate from 3 percent to 6 percent and will keep it at 6 percent for ten consecutive years. To illustrate the effect of increased interest rate payments produced by higher interest rates on the national debt over time, I use the nice round number $10 trillion as an example. The table includes the dollar amount taxpayers will have to pay to fund the debt at the higher rate in each of the ten years. Table 2.1 shows that the higher rate will affect $4.13 trillion of the debt in the first year, $5.56 trillion in the second year, and so on.

TABLE 2.1. Dollar amounts of a $10 trillion national debt that will be affected by rate changes each year

Year 1	$4.13	Year 6	$8.51
Year 2	$5.56	Year 7	$8.83
Year 3	$6.99	Year 8	$8.97
Year 4	$7.59	Year 9	$9.12
Year 5	$8.19	Year 10	$9.27

Note: All figures in trillions.

The second table, table 2.2, shows how I arrived at the numbers. This table also illustrates the composition of the debt—for example, what percentage of the debt is comprised of Treasury bills; what percentage of it is comprised of three-year, five-year, seven-year, and ten-year notes; and what percentage is comprised of the thirty-year bond. The longer the term of the security, the higher interest rate the security will pay. This is commonly referred to as the "yield curve."

TABLE 2.2. Dollar amount of rate changes by security type: hypothetical $10 trillion debt

Maturity Period	Percent of Nat. Debt	$ Amount in Trillions	Year 1	Year 2	Year 3	Year 4	Year 5	Year 6	Year 7	Year 8	Year 9	Year 10
1 Yr. T-Bill	27%	$2.700	$2.700	$2.700	$2.700	$2.700	$2.700	$2.700	$2.700	$2.700	$2.700	$2.700
3 Yr. Treas	25%	$2.500	$0.833	$1.666	$2.500	$2.500	$2.500	$2.500	$2.500	$2.500	$2.500	$2.500
5 Yr. Treas	14%	$1.400	$0.280	$0.560	$0.840	$1.120	$1.400	$1.400	$1.400	$1.400	$1.400	$1.400
7 Yr. Treas	12%	$1.200	$0.171	$0.343	$0.514	$0.686	$0.857	$1.029	$1.200	$1.200	$1.200	$1.200
10 Yr. Treas	11%	$1.100	$0.110	$0.220	$0.330	$0.440	$0.550	$0.660	$0.770	$0.880	$0.990	$1.100
30 Yr. Treas.	11%	$1.100	$0.037	$0.073	$0.110	$0.147	$0.183	$0.220	$0.257	$0.293	$0.330	$0.367
	Totals											
Totals	100%	$10.000	$4.131	$5.562	$6.994	$7.592	$8.190	$8.509	$8.827	$8.973	$9.120	$9.267

Note: This table accounts for 92.7 percent of the $10 trillion debt. The 7.3 percent not rolled (reissued) comes from the twenty years remaining on the thirty-year bond, which will continue to pay the original interest rate.

The doubling of interest rates will not immediately result in the doubling of debt-interest payments. As I previously stated, the Treasury issues securities each year to fund new debt and to replace existing debt that was rolled over. Only the newly issued securities will reflect the higher interest rate.

Table 2.3 shows that 41 percent of the existing national debt will be rolled over in the first year, 70 percent by year three, about 82 percent by year five, and so on. A closer review of the data shows that 100 percent of the Treasury bills will be rolled over in the first year in addition to one-third of three-year notes, 20 percent of five-year notes, 10 percent of ten-year notes, and so on. In total, about 93 percent of all existing debt will be rolled over in ten years.

TABLE 2.3. Percentage of the national debt affected
by rate changes by year

Year 1	41.3 percent	Year 6	85.1 percent
Year 2	55.6 percent	Year 7	88.3 percent
Year 3	69.9 percent	Year 8	89.7 percent
Year 4	75.9 percent	Year 9	91.2 percent
Year 5	81.9 percent	Year 10	92.7 percent

It is next to impossible to predict how much the national debt will grow in the coming years and what the interest on that debt will be. Some of the factors that affect these numbers include the following:

- the president's and Congress's political will to control government spending and limit reliance on national debt increases to fund budget deficits
- the strength of the economy, the unemployment rate, and other economic indicators
- the timing and size of the Federal Reserve's interest-rate changes
- unforeseen international events

Early in 2010, the nonpartisan Congressional Budget Office (CBO) predicted a ten-year increase in the national debt totaling $8.5 trillion, equating to an average yearly increase of $850 billion.

$1 Trillion, Please!

In the near future, the government will be asking taxpayers to fork up more than $1 trillion a year just to pay the interest on the national debt, and the problem is only going to get worse.

Please carefully review table 2.4. It starts with the current $18 trillion national debt. I assume the Fed will raise the average rate to 6 percent from the current 3 percent and hold it steady for ten years. I also assume the government will add $750 billion to the national debt each year to cover budget shortfalls. (In the first four years of the Obama administration, the national debt grew by about $1.25 trillion a year.) Table 2.5 makes the same assumptions, except I use a 5 percent interest rate instead of the 6 percent rate. The tables show that at 6 percent, the annual interest on the national debt will reach *$1 trillion in 2018*, and at 5 percent it would reach *$1 trillion in 2020*.

TABLE 2.4. Annual debt interest—6 percent interest rate: $750 billion annual debt increases

	Beginning Debt	Percent at Old Rate (3%)	Dollar Amt Old Rate (3%)	Interest Amount (3%)	Percent at New Rate (6%)	Dollar Amt New Rate (6%)	Interest Amount (6%)	Annual Debt Amt Increase	Int on New Debt (6%)	Total Debt	Total Interest (6%)
2015	$18,000	100.0%	$18,000	$540	0.0%	$0	$0	$0	$0	$18,000	$540
2016	$18,000	58.7%	$10,566	$317	41.3%	$7,434	$446	$750	$45	$18,750	$808
2017	$18,000	44.4%	$7,992	$240	55.6%	$10,008	$600	$1,500	$90	$19,500	$930
2018	$18,000	30.1%	$5,418	$163	69.9%	$12,582	$755	$2,250	$135	$20,250	$1,052
2019	$18,000	24.1%	$4,338	$130	75.9%	$13,662	$820	$3,000	$180	$21,000	$1,130
2020	$18,000	18.1%	$3,258	$98	81.9%	$14,742	$885	$3,750	$225	$21,750	$1,207
2021	$18,000	14.9%	$2,682	$80	85.1%	$15,318	$919	$4,500	$270	$22,500	$1,270
2022	$18,000	11.7%	$2,106	$63	88.3%	$15,894	$954	$5,250	$315	$23,250	$1,332
2023	$18,000	10.3%	$1,854	$56	89.7%	$16,146	$969	$6,000	$360	$24,000	$1,384
2024	$18,000	8.8%	$1,584	$48	91.2%	$16,416	$985	$6,750	$405	$24,750	$1,437
2025	$18,000	7.3%	$1,314	$39	92.7%	$16,686	$1,001	$7,500	$450	$25,500	$1,452

Note: The total interest on the debt reaches $1.052 trillion in 2018.

TABLE 2.5. Annual debt interest—5 percent interest rate: $750 billion annual debt increases

	Beginning Debt	Percent at Old Rate (3%)	Dollar Amt Old Rate (3%)	Interest Amount (3%)	Percent at New Rate (5%)	Dollar Amt New Rate (5%)	Interest Amount (5%)	Annual Debt Amt Increase	Int. on New Debt (5%)	Total Debt	Total Interest (5%)
2015	$18,000	100.0%	$18,000	$540	0.0%	$0	$0	$0	$0	$18,000	$540
2016	$18,000	58.7%	$10,566	$317	41.3%	$7,434	$372	$750	$38	$18,750	$726
2017	$18,000	44.4%	$7,992	$240	55.6%	$10,008	$500	$1,500	$75	$19,500	$815
2018	$18,000	30.1%	$5,418	$163	69.9%	$12,582	$629	$2,250	$113	$20,250	$904
2019	$18,000	24.1%	$4,338	$130	75.9%	$13,662	$683	$3,000	$150	$21,000	$963
2020	$18,000	18.1%	$3,258	$98	81.9%	$14,742	$737	$3,750	$188	$21,750	$1,022
2021	$18,000	14.9%	$2,682	$80	85.1%	$15,318	$766	$4,500	$225	$22,500	$1,071
2022	$18,000	11.7%	$2,106	$63	88.3%	$15,894	$795	$5,250	$263	$23,250	$1,120
2023	$18,000	10.3%	$1,854	$56	89.7%	$16,146	$807	$6,000	$300	$24,000	$1,163
2024	$18,000	8.8%	$1,584	$48	91.2%	$16,416	$821	$6,750	$338	$24,750	$1,206
2025	$18,000	7.3%	$1,314	$39	92.7%	$16,686	$834	$7,500	$375	$25,500	$1,249

Note: the total interest on the debt reaches $1.022 trillion in 2020.

Because the national debt is so huge, it's interesting to note what effect the 1 percent increase from a 5 percent rate and a 6 percent rate would make. In the first year alone, the higher rate would add $82 billion to the annual debt-interest payment, ($808 billion vs. $726 billion), and by the tenth year the number would jump to $242 billion. ($1,491 billion vs. $1,249 billion) The combined increase over the entire ten-year period would be more than $1.8 trillion.

Fact or Fiction?

The numbers I used in the tables are, of course, only estimates and my best guesses on how this issue will play out. But there is a wide range of opinions out there on the projected growth of the national debt and on what the Federal Reserve is likely to do with interest rates over the next decade.

I estimate interest rates for the next decade will range between 4 percent and 6 percent if inflation stays tame. Estimates of how much the government will need to borrow to make up for budget shortfalls range from $400 billion to as high as $1 trillion. In order to get the best-possible understanding of how government borrowing and interest rate changes affect the amount of interest taxpayers will have to pay to fund the national debt, it is best to review a wide range of scenarios. Tables 2.6–2.9 illustrate how much debt interest would be required under all these conditions.

TABLE 2.6. National debt interest with $400 billion annual deficits

Year	Interest Rate of 4%		Interest Rate of 5%		Interest Rate of 8%		Interest Rate of 10%		Interest Rate of 12%	
	Nat'l Debt Amount	Annual Int Amt	Nat'l Debt Amount	Annual Int Amt	Nat'l Debt Amount	Annual Int Amt	Nat'l Debt Amount	Annual Int Amt	Nat'l Debt Amount	Annual Int Amt
2015	$18,000	$720	$18,000	$1,080	$18,000	$1,440	$18,000	$1,800	$18,000	$2,160
2016	$18,400	$735	$18,400	$1,104	$18,400	$1,472	$18,400	$1,840	$18,400	$2,208
2017	$18,800	$752	$18,800	$1,128	$18,800	$1,504	$18,800	$1,880	$18,800	$2,256
2018	$19,200	$768	$19,200	$1,152	$19,200	$1,536	$19,200	$1,920	$19,200	$2,304
2019	$19,500	$784	$19,500	$1,176	$19,500	$1,568	$19,500	$1,960	$19,500	$2,352
2020	$20,000	$800	$20,000	$1,200	$20,000	$1,600	$20,000	$2,000	$20,000	$2,400
2021	$20,400	$816	$20,400	$1,224	$20,400	$1,632	$20,400	$2,040	$20,400	$2,448
2022	$20,800	$832	$20,800	$1,248	$20,800	$1,664	$20,800	$2,080	$20,800	$2,496
2023	$21,200	$848	$21,200	$1,272	$21,200	$1,696	$21,200	$2,120	$21,200	$2,544
2024	$21,600	$864	$21,600	$1,296	$21,600	$1,728	$21,600	$2,160	$21,600	$2,592
2025	$22,000	$880	$22,000	$1,320	$22,000	$1,760	$22,000	$2,200	$22,000	$2,640

In Billions

TABLE 2.7. National debt interest with $600 billion annual deficits

Year	Interest Rate of 4%		Interest Rate of 5%		Interest Rate of 8%		Interest Rate of 10%		Interest Rate of 12%	
	Nat'l Debt Amount	Annual Int Amt	Nat'l Debt Amount	Annual Int Amt	Nat'l Debt Amount	Annual Int Amt	Nat'l Debt Amount	Annual Int Amt	Nat'l Debt Amount	Annual Int Amt
2015	$18,000	$720	$18,000	$1,080	$18,000	$1,440	$18,000	$1,800	$18,000	$2,160
2016	$18,600	$744	$18,600	$1,116	$18,600	$1,488	$18,600	$1,860	$18,600	$2,232
2017	$19,200	$768	$19,200	$1,152	$19,200	$1,536	$19,200	$1,920	$19,200	$2,304
2018	$19,800	$792	$19,800	$1,188	$19,800	$1,584	$19,800	$1,980	$19,800	$2,376
2019	$20,400	$816	$20,400	$1,224	$20,400	$1,632	$20,400	$2,040	$20,400	$2,448
2020	$21,000	$840	$21,000	$1,260	$21,000	$1,680	$21,000	$2,100	$21,000	$2,520
2021	$21,600	$864	$21,600	$1,296	$21,600	$1,728	$21,600	$2,160	$21,600	$2,592
2022	$22,200	$888	$22,200	$1,332	$22,200	$1,776	$22,200	$2,220	$22,200	$2,664
2023	$22,800	$912	$22,800	$1,368	$22,800	$1,824	$22,800	$2,280	$22,800	$2,736
2024	$23,400	$936	$23,400	$1,404	$23,400	$1,872	$23,400	$2,340	$23,400	$2,808
2025	$24,000	$960	$24,000	$1,440	$24,000	$1,920	$24,000	$2,400	$24,000	$2,880

In Billions

TABLE 2.8. National debt interest with $800 billion annual deficits

	National Debt Interest with $800 Billion Annual Deficits									
	Interest Rate of 4%		Interest Rate of 6%		Interest Rate of 8%		Interest Rate of 10%		Interest Rate of 12%	
Year	Nat'l Debt Amount	Annual Int Amt	Nat'l Debt Amount	Annual Int Amt	Nat'l Debt Amount	Annual Int Amt	Nat'l Debt Amount	Annual Int Amt	Nat'l Debt Amount	Annual Int Amt
2015	$18,000	$720	$18,000	$1,080	$18,000	$1,440	$18,000	$1,800	$18,000	$2,160
2016	$18,800	$752	$18,800	$1,128	$18,800	$1,504	$18,800	$1,880	$18,800	$2,256
2017	$19,600	$784	$19,600	$1,176	$19,600	$1,568	$19,600	$1,960	$19,600	$2,352
2018	$20,400	$816	$20,400	$1,224	$20,400	$1,632	$20,400	$2,040	$20,400	$2,448
2019	$21,200	$848	$21,200	$1,272	$21,200	$1,696	$21,200	$2,120	$21,200	$2,544
2020	$22,000	$880	$22,000	$1,320	$22,000	$1,760	$22,000	$2,200	$22,000	$2,640
2021	$22,800	$912	$22,800	$1,368	$22,800	$1,824	$22,800	$2,280	$22,800	$2,736
2022	$23,600	$944	$23,600	$1,416	$23,600	$1,888	$23,600	$2,360	$23,600	$2,832
2023	$24,400	$975	$24,400	$1,464	$24,400	$1,952	$24,400	$2,440	$24,400	$2,928
2024	$25,200	$1,008	$25,200	$1,512	$25,200	$2,016	$25,200	$2,520	$25,200	$3,024
2025	$26,000	$1,040	$26,000	$1,560	$26,000	$2,080	$26,000	$2,600	$26,000	$3,120

In Billions

TABLE 2.9. National debt interest with $1 trillion annual deficits

	National Debt Interest with $1 trillion Annual Deficits									
	Interest Rate of 4%		Interest Rate of 6%		Interest Rate of 8%		Interest Rate of 10%		Interest Rate of 12%	
Year	Nat'l Debt Amount	Annual Int Amt	Nat'l Debt Amount	Annual Int Amt	Nat'l Debt Amount	Annual Int Amt	Nat'l Debt Amount	Annual Int Amt	Nat'l Debt Amount	Annual Int Amt
2015	$18,000	$720	$18,000	$1,080	$18,000	$1,440	$18,000	$1,800	$18,000	$2,160
2016	$19,000	$760	$19,000	$1,140	$19,000	$1,520	$19,000	$1,900	$19,000	$2,280
2017	$20,000	$800	$20,000	$1,200	$20,000	$1,600	$20,000	$2,000	$20,000	$2,400
2018	$21,000	$840	$21,000	$1,260	$21,000	$1,680	$21,000	$2,100	$21,000	$2,520
2019	$22,000	$880	$22,000	$1,320	$22,000	$1,760	$22,000	$2,200	$22,000	$2,640
2020	$23,000	$920	$23,000	$1,380	$23,000	$1,840	$23,000	$2,300	$23,000	$2,760
2021	$24,000	$960	$24,000	$1,440	$24,000	$1,920	$24,000	$2,400	$24,000	$2,880
2022	$25,000	$1,000	$25,000	$1,500	$25,000	$2,000	$25,000	$2,500	$25,000	$3,000
2023	$26,000	$1,040	$26,000	$1,560	$26,000	$2,080	$26,000	$2,600	$26,000	$3,120
2024	$27,000	$1,080	$27,000	$1,620	$27,000	$2,160	$27,000	$2,700	$27,000	$3,240
2025	$28,000	$1,120	$28,000	$1,680	$28,000	$2,240	$28,000	$2,800	$28,000	$3,360

In Billions

Just a reminder! The average interest rate over the last fifty years was over 6 percent. Use your own estimates of how high the debt will be and where interest rates will be over the next decade, and make your own calculations of how much interest taxpayers will have to fork over. All the information you need to do that is available in these tables.

Is it not obvious that it won't be long before our annual budget includes trillion-dollar debt payments? What may not be so obvious is that such payments will add hundreds of billions to the budget deficit. You can be sure there will be very little in spending cuts or tax increases to offset any increase in debt interest. Therefore, by default, our government will deal with this problem simply by adding it to the national debt. It looks like the national debt is becoming a perpetual problem that is getting worse every year!

The Federal Reserve's Effect on Debts and Deficits

In 2001, US taxpayers paid $359 billion in interest on a national debt of less than $6 trillion. Fast-forward eleven years to 2012. The national debt was at $16 trillion, yet the interest on the debt was only $342 billion. How is it possible that the interest on the $16 trillion debt was less than the interest on the $6 trillion debt? The answer has to do with the Federal Reserve.

After the start of the 2008 recession, the Federal Reserve began an extended period of record-low interest rates. Former fed chairman Ben Bernanke pushed this policy in order to stimulate an economy that was undergoing a recession. It's been seven years since the Fed started this quantitative-easing policy, and it has little to show for it. Economic growth averaged less than 2 percent over the period and employment remained stagnant. In both areas, the economic results fell well short of the targets the president set and are especially disappointing when factoring in the $787 billion stimulus package Congress approved in 2009. At best, the Fed can claim credit for stopping the recession and stabilizing the job market. However, most of the Fed's actions that accomplished this were instituted in the first few months of the recession.

In my opinion, the Fedv's low interest rate policy has had some major unintended beneficial consequences on the size of the budget deficit and the size of the national debt. Over the last twenty-four years, the US government paid an average of 5 percent interest on the Treasury securities that comprise the national debt. But, as I previously stated, that 5 percent rate undercounts the real average interest rate of 5.8 percent. Bear in mind that even though the Fed's low-rate policy resulted in a major reduction in the amount of interest needed to fund the debt that was not its intention. The Fed's action was strictly for economic reasons, solely to fight the recession by stimulating the economy, as low rates make it easier for corporations to borrow money to expand. Had the Fed instead raised rates to fight inflation, the interest rates on the debt would have increased.

The national debt is so huge that the 0.008 percent difference between the 5 and 5.8 percent figures I just cited would have made more than a $500 billion difference in the amount of debt interest paid over the last five years.

The Cost of the Fed's Low Rate Policy

As previously stated the average interest rate paid on the debt for the twenty years up to 2007 was 5.8 percent. But in the seven-year period since the 2008 recession, the Fed cut rates literally in half, averaging only 2.88 percent. Take a look at table 2.10 to see the actual interest paid and national debt incurred.

TABLE 2.10. Interest rates as a result of the Fed's low-rate policy

Year	Actual interest paid	National debt	Interest rate
2014	$431	$17,824	2.42%
2013	$416	$16,738	2.49%
2012	$360	$16,066	2.24%
2011	$454	$14,790	3.07%
2010	$413	$13,562	3.05%
2009	$383	$11,990	3.19%
2008	$451	$10,025	4.50%
Totals		$2,908	2.8%

Source: Treasury Direct

There's no question the Fed successfully and dramatically brought down interest rates, even if it fell short of its goal of stimulating the economy. The low rates brought down the borrowing cost for businesses and lowered mortgage rates for potential home buyers. However, they devastated those who counted on interest as their main source of income. On the surface it looks like a simple, riskless solution to a major problem. But is that really the case?

The Fed buys and sells tens of billions of dollars in bonds when it wants to raise or lower interest rates by 0.25 percent—its most common action when it wants to boost or slow the economy. Bond traders often invest when they believe they will make profits from anticipating the Fed's next move on rates. Changing economic conditions are an important factor in bond trading because they affect the Fed's judgment on where interest rates should be. In other words, bond traders are sometimes able to get ahead of the Fed, which meets only eight times a year to discuss rate changes. Bond traders trade daily and can cause interest rate moves through trading activity, and sometimes the Fed needs to play catch-up.

How Does the Fed Manage Rate Changes?

The Fed's most common procedure for changing the interest rate is first to announce its intention to reduce (or increase) rates. That statement alone stops bond traders in their tracks. Bond traders live by the credo "Don't fight the Fed." The power of the Fed trumps the power of any institution. When lowering rates, the Fed goes on a massive bond-buying binge to solidify its policy. As of June 2015, the Federal Reserve owned a massive $4 trillion in Treasury and mortgage-backed securities.

A Free Lunch for the Fed?

In an effort to keep downward pressure on interest rates, the Fed purchased $40 billion a month in mortgage-backed securities and $45 billion a month in ten-year treasuries. It used $4 trillion of taxpayer money to push down interest rates. What it got for the $4 trillion was $4 trillion worth of Treasury and mortgage-backed securities. Sounds reasonable!

So what's the problem? If the Fed is successful in reviving the economy, it will be stuck with major losses when it attempts to liquidate that $4 trillion worth of securities. For example, the ten-year Treasury bonds are yielding about 2.1 percent (as of late October 2015). If the economy returns to normal, these bonds would yield 5 percent or more. If the Fed wants to liquidate its bond positions, it would have to sell them well below their purchase price and take a loss in the tens of billions of dollars—for the taxpayers will absorb.

There is an alternative. The Fed could just hold on to the securities, collect the periodic interest payments, and collect the principals at maturity. The only problem I can see is that this would tie up lots money for ten years or more. If this is correct, then I guess the Fed can have its free lunch, but I don't believe it has the power to buy unlimited amounts of securities and the ability to keep interest rates artificially low indefinitely. I believe at some point, market forces must enter the picture, but I don't know where, when, or how (remember Greece, Spain, and Italy).

The Conning of America

In my opinion, this is the biggest con game in the history of humanity. The US government borrows $18 trillion by selling government securities to investors and then buys back its own securities in the open market. It's the equivalent of having a shill at an auction.

The Federal Reserve is, in fact, manipulating the bond market. In America, manipulating the price of any product available to the public is illegal—that is, illegal for everyone except the Federal Reserve. This is a joke! I can't think of a single product on planet earth that has a market value higher than the US national debt. Yet the government entity responsible for insuring the economic wellness of the nation is permitted to peddle trillions of dollars' worth of bonds at a price different from its true market value.

The purpose of the Fed's action is to force down interest rates (and thereby "accommodate" the economy) by buying bonds en masse. Buying the bonds puts upward pressure on their price and simultaneously puts downward pressure on their yield (interest rate). For example, if you buy a bond with a 3 percent interest rate and pay "par" (100 percent of its face value), you will receive $3 in interest annually on every $100 invested, or a 3 percent yield. Let's say the Fed buys enough of this same bond to push the price up to 150 percent of its face value. The purchaser would receive the same $3 in interest on a $150 investment, or a 2 percent yield. This equates to the Federal Reserve lowering the interest rate from 3 percent to 2 percent because the Fed can now issue new $100 bonds at a 2 percent interest rate.

Here we are, a country founded on free market principles, and we allow the Federal Reserve to bully the bond market and force investors who invest in US treasuries worldwide to accept a security with a "manufactured" interest rate. As mentioned elsewhere in this book, a mere hint from the Federal Reserve that it was going to slowly reduce the monthly bond-buying program that supports low interest rates rocked the bond market and sent rates up 50 percent in one week. In my opinion, this spike in rates reflects the skepticism bond investors feel about the true market value of these government securities. It is likely they believe that without the support of the massive bond-buying program by the Federal Reserve, the bonds would carry a substantially higher interest rate and lower market value. Investors who own long-term government securities will likely suffer substantial losses with the return to "normal" interest rates. The longer the maturity of the bond, the more severe the potential loss.

There are a lot-safer investments than lending the US government billions of dollars for thirty years at 4 percent or for ten years at 3 percent. The lengths the Federal Reserve is willing to go to push down interest rates is astonishing. Since the start of the quantitative-easing program from November 2008 through January 2014, the Fed purchased over $4 trillion in securities. That's more than all the tax revenues the United States collected from individuals and corporations in 2015 (an estimated $3.2 trillion). Those who support this policy would argue that the Fed is doing exactly what it should be doing—executing a monetary policy that will help stimulate a sagging economy. Of course this is true. With an $18 trillion national debt and budget deficits averaging a trillion a year for each of the last six years, is at any wonder that the credit rating of the United States is going down the toilet and that our economy is not up to par?

The Federal Reserve's $4 trillion in bond purchases over the last four years is a stark admission that interest rates on treasuries would be substantially higher if they were allowed to trade freely in the open market. If this were not true, there would be no need for Fed intervention. It is extremely important that concerned Americans understand that all markets where securities are traded function purely on perception. That is, a stock or bond is worth X because it meets a certain set of parameters unique to each investor. There are a zillion financial analysts out there that will provide you with charts and graphs that show what a stock or bond should sell at based on their own sets of parameters. In my opinion, these analysts have very little value. Market sentiment or perception trumps any chart or graph. Simply stated, it is presumed all stocks and bonds trade at fair market value because the buyer and seller exchange cash for securities at a mutually agreed-upon price. When you purchase a security, the seller is not doing you a favor; he or she is happy to get rid of the security at the price you are willing to pay for it, believing the money could be better used elsewhere. When you sell your security, the buyer is willing to take it off your hands in the belief that the money is being invested wisely in the stock you are selling.

Market perception can change dramatically as evidenced by the dot-com bust of 1999–2001, when a household name like Amazon.com dropped from $107 a share to $8 a share or when a bellwether like Cisco Systems lost more than 80 percent of its value. As a matter of fact, as shown in figure 2.3, the slide in the tech-heavy NASDAQ was so severe—from March 2000 through October 2002, the index dropped from 5,046 to 1,108—that the average loss for all listed stocks exceeded 80 percent. Amazon.com and Cisco Systems continued to prosper as companies, but investors suddenly took on the herd mentality and rushed for the exits. This is a stark illustration of how market perception can change in a relatively short period of time and have devastating consequences.

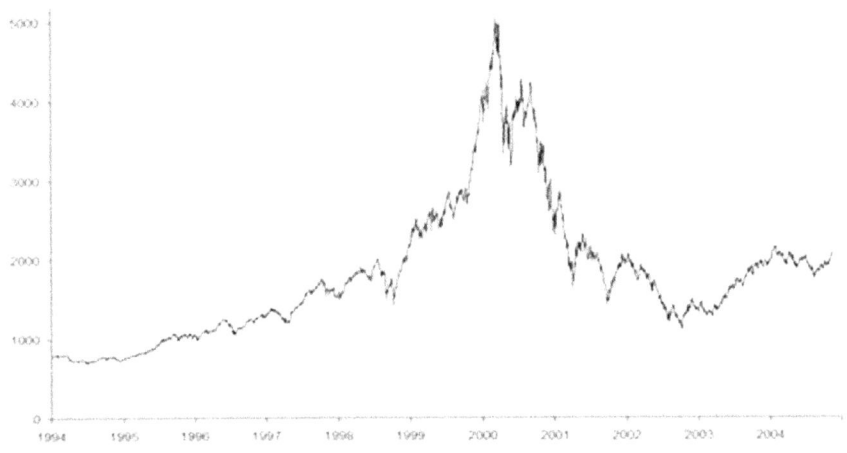

Figure 2.3. NASDAQ Composite, 1994–2004

At the high and at the low of the slide, the NASDAQ-listed securities traded at their fair market value, unencumbered by any outside influences. This was not the case with US government securities because of the hanky-panky on the part of the Federal Reserve resulting from their quantitative-easing program. In my opinion, continued massive purchases of government securities is creating a pressure bubble by forcibly keeping prices up and interest rates down. The pressure is steadily building because of the growing national debt, continued deficit spending, and the declining creditworthiness of the United States. When the Fed opens this pressure valve, whether forcibly or voluntarily, interest rates will probably rise sharply and start a series of events with severe negative economic and social consequences. For lack of a better term, I'll call it the possible "bursting of the interest rate bubble."

As of January 2014, investors in government securities owned about $1.5 trillion in thirty-year Treasury bonds, yielding less than 4 percent. and almost $8 trillion in Treasury notes, yielding from 1 percent to 3 percent. In my opinion, the primary reason investors are willing to accept these low yields is that they take comfort from the Federal Reserve's bond-buying program, which insures sustained low rates and protects their market value. In any case, Treasury securities are a liquid asset and investors can liquidate their positions at will.

I believe that rates will rise, possibly substantially, once the Fed ends it bond-buying program and moves away from its aggressive low-rate policy. As with the dot-com bust, putting a value on any asset is a mindset, and when investors wake up to the fact that the financial condition of the United States is in tatters, higher interest rates are almost a certainty.

It doesn't take a PhD in economics to identify this problem. All the data needed to support this issue are in the public domain. Nor does it take a PhD in economics to bring this issue to the forefront. All that it takes is a competent and unbiased media. However, it will surely take a PhD in economics to resolve the economic issues our country faces right now, much less under a crisis scenario that will feature trillion-dollar debt interest payments, higher interest rates, and a ballooning national debt. There is no doubt in my mind that the president and Congress come up a little short in the area of economics.

The Federal Reserve and Fighting Inflation

Can the Federal Reserve attack inflation with the same intensity it did during the hyperinflation years from 1976 to 1985? As shown in table 2.11, the average inflation rate over that ten-year period exceeded 7 percent, peaking in the three-year period between 1979 and 1981, when it averaged more than 11 percent. To combat that hyperinflation, the Fed, led by Paul Volcker, raised both short-term and long-term rates to 13 percent. The inflation rate over the most recent seven-year period averaged just under 2 percent.

TABLE 2.11.

Inflation and Interest Rates 1976 – 1985

	Inflation Rate CPI		1-Year T-Bill Rate		10 Year Bond Rate
1976	5.80%	1976	5.88%	1976	7.61%
1977	6.50%	1977	6.08%	1977	7.42%
1978	7.60%	1978	8.34%	1978	8.41%
1979	11.30%	1979	10.65%	1979	9.43%
1980	*13.50%*	*1980*	*12.00%*	*1980*	*11.43%*
1981	*10.30%*	*1981*	*14.80%*	*1981*	*13.92%*
1982	*6.20%*	*1982*	*12.27%*	*1982*	*13.01%*
1983	3.20%	1983	9.58%	1983	11.10%
1984	4.30%	1984	10.91%	1984	12.46%
1985	3.60%	1985	8.42%	1985	10.62%
Average	7.22%		9.90%		10.54%

The United States is a much different country economically than it was during those hyperinflation years. The national debt is now at $18 trillion, more than fifteen times greater than it was during those years. Over that ten-year period, the national debt averaged $1.1 trillion, and debt interest averaged only $67 billion a year. Table 2.12 illustrates the size of the annual national debt and debt interest paid over that period.

TABLE 2.12. Size of annual national debt and interest paid on the during the hyperinflation years, 1976–1985

Year	Pres	Debt Interest	Nat'l Debt	Interest Rate	Year	Pres.	Debt Interest	Nat'l Debt	Interest Rate
1985	Reagan	$129	$1.945	6.63%	1980	Carter	$52	$930	5.59%
1984	Reagan	$111	$1.662	6.68%	1979	Carter	$43	$845	5.09%
1983	Reagan	$89	$1.410	6.31%	1978	Carter	$35	$789	4.44%
1982	Reagan	$85	$1.197	7.10%	1977	Carter	$30	$719	4.17%
1981	Reagan	$69	$1.029	6.71%	1976	Ford	$27	$654	4.13%
In Billions					10 Year Average		$67	$1.120	5.98%

The average interest rates paid on the national debt jumped from 4.2 percent in 1977 to 7.1 in 1982—almost a 60 percent increase. This is an example of how long it takes for Fed action on interest rates to affect interest on the national debt. The purpose of the Fed's action was to tame inflation. Raising the amount of interest the government has to pay to fund the national debt is the last thing the Fed wants to do because the debt has to be funded from tax revenues.

From 1981 through 2013, inflation increased by 280 percent, while the national debt increased by 1,500 percent. Tables 2.13 and 2.14 show the US budget during these years going up to the year 2018. The future budgets are the CBO's estimates.

TABLE 2.13. US budget, 1976–1985 (hyperinflation years)

	1976	1977	1978	1979	1980	1981	1982	1983	1984	1985
Pensions	$81	$94	$104	$117	$134	$158	$176	$189	$197	$206
Health Care	$32	$37	$41	$47	$55	$66	$74	$81	$88	$99
Education	$20	$22	$28	$32	$33	$35	$28	$28	$29	$31
Defense	$115	$122	$131	$144	$168	$194	$222	$247	$269	$295
Welfare	$42	$40	$38	$39	$55	$64	$68	$81	$70	$85
Protection	$2	$2	$2	$2	$3	$3	$3	$4	$4	$4
Transportation	$14	$15	$16	$18	$21	$21	$21	$21	$24	$26
General Government	$12	$15	$14	$14	$15	$14	$13	$14	$14	$14
Other Spending	$29	$34	$50	$48	$93	$53	$56	$54	$47	$57
Interest	$27	$30	$36	$43	$53	$69	$85	$90	$111	$130
Total Spending	$372	$409	$459	$504	$591	$678	$746	$808	$852	$948
Federal Deficit	$74	$54	$59	$41	$74	$79	$128	$208	$185	$212
Gross Public Debt	$629	$706	$777	$830	$909	$995	$1,137	$1,372	$1,568	$1,817

TABLE 2.14. US budget, 2013–2018

	2013	2014	2015	2016	2017	2018
Pensions	$874.3	$928.5	$980.2	$1,037.4	$1,093.9	$1,151.0
Health Care	$882.2	$973.6	$1,058.0	$1,141.8	$1,174.0	$1,211.5
Education	$98.0	$141.8	$119.4	$119.4	$126.5	$133.5
Defense	$856.5	$830.9	$823.2	$811.6	$812.5	$815.4
Welfare	$422.4	$393.7	$384.6	$387.9	$384.9	$382.9
Protection	$37.0	$36.0	$36.5	$37.1	$37.9	$38.7
Transportation	$94.5	$103.8	$115.8	$111.8	$109.9	$111.8
General Government	$55.9	$53.4	$54.2	$57.6	$57.5	$60.4
Other Spending	$141.4	$93.2	$82.7	$85.2	$76.9	$82.4
Interest	$222.8	$222.9	$253.6	$300.1	$373.4	$461.5
Total Spending	$3,685.0	$3,777.8	$3,908.2	$4,089.9	$4,247.4	$4,449.1
Federal Deficit	$972.9	$741.2	$576.5	$528.4	$486.9	$475.3
Gross Public Debt	$17,249.3	$18,246.9	$19,147.8	$20,026.6	$20,876.5	$21,696.2

In the two hundred years from 1776 to 1976, the national debt went from $0 to $629 billion. In the next nine years, from 1976 to 1985, it tripled to $1.8 trillion. I assume the era of reliance on deficit spending without increasing taxes as a routine way of funding programs began around that time, and I guess the politicians felt a debt load of $629 billion was easily manageable. After all, $629 billion was less than two times that year's spending, as compared to 2013, when the debt load was more than four times that year's spending. (For various reasons the actual amount of debt interest was about 10–15 percent higher than it appears in the budget.)

A comparison of the 1976 and 2013 budgets, as shown in table 2.15, highlights some changes that have taken place in how the government prioritizes the spending of tax revenues. The four items listed show that defense spending dropped by 18 percent, spending on health care tripled, government employee pensions grew about 5 percent, and welfare costs remained stable.

As the table shows, in 2013, pensions, health care, and defense each accounted for more than 30 percent of revenues. When you add in welfare, these four budget items alone amounted to 111 percent of tax revenues. When you add in the remaining budget items, spending reached 126 percent of revenues; thus a $973 billion budget deficit and a $973 billion addition were incurred for the national debt for this year.

TABLE 2.15. Comparison of budget priorities
between 1976 and 2013

	1976				2013			
	Spending	Amount	Percent of Revenues	Percent of Total Spend	Spending	Amount	Percent of Revenues	Percent of Total Spend
Pensions	$298	$81	27.14%	21.76%	$3,685	$874	32.24%	23.73%
Health Care	$298	$32	10.60%	8.50%	$3,685	$882	32.53%	23.94%
Defense	$298	$115	38.41%	30.80%	$3,685	$857	31.58%	23.24%
Welfare	$298	$42	14.12%	11.32%	$3,685	$422	15.57%	11.46%
Totals			90.27%	72.38%			111.92%	82.37%

Fighting Inflation Ain't What It Used to Be

If the Fed were to adopt a moderate "anti-inflation" stance and raise interest rates to around 8 percent and then immediately apply that 8 percent increase to the 2014 national debt of $18 trillion, it would increase the annual debt interest to about $1.44 trillion. But, as I previously explained, it takes time for rate changes to work their way to the bottom line. The amount $1.44 trillion is a $1.09 trillion increase over the 2012 budget deficit of $342 billion. Forty-one percent of that rate increase will take effect after one year, boosting the debt-interest payments from $342 to $792 billion, and after three years to more than $1 trillion. These figures do not include additional debt-interest payments from any increases in deficit spending incurred during this period.

The debt-interest increase to $792 billion (8 percent at end of year one) is almost one-fifth of the 2012 budget of $3.7 trillion and more than one-quarter of total tax revenues of $2.6 trillion. In other words, under this scenario, after one year, 25 percent of all tax revenues would go toward funding the national debt.

Any effort by the Federal Reserve to fight inflation through a high-interest-rate policy will be substantially more difficult than it was during those hyperinflation years. The reason is, of course, the national debt, which is not the only problem, but it is far and away the biggest one. In order to illustrate this point, I created two tables to show how tax revenues, government spending, budget deficits, and debt interest all contribute to the growth of the national debt. Table 2.16 is for the hyperinflation years 1976 through 1985. Table 2.17 is for the current period from 2009 to 2018.

The Federal Reserve's aggressive action to fight hyperinflation caused unemployment to jump from under 6 percent to almost 11 percent over a three-year period from 1980 to 1983, as shown in figure 2.4. The damage that similar interest rate moves will have on today's economy is, of course, unknown, but you can be sure it won't be pretty.

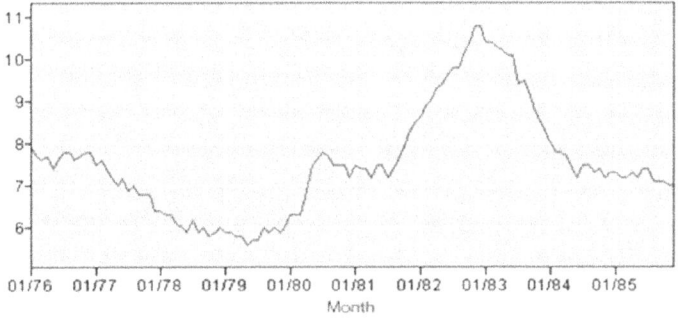

Figure 2.4. Unemployment rate for 1976–1985, the hyperinflation years.

Source: Bureau of Labor Statistics

The 1 Percent Factor, Part One

In my opinion this last point is the primary reason the national debt problem is so misunderstood. The interest on an $18 trillion debt costs taxpayers $180 billion for every one-percentage-point hike in the interest rate. For example, a sustained 5.8 percent rate would cost taxpayers $1.04

trillion annually. (Remember, 5.8 percent is close to the average rate over the last four decades).

Because of the low-rate policy put into effect to boost the economy after the 2008 recession, debt interest averaged $220 billion and exceeded $300 billion only once from then to the present. The low-rate policy enabled the president and Congress to downplay the severity of the national debt problem, successfully keeping the issue out of the public eye. During this period, the national debt rose from just over $10 trillion to the present (October 2015) figure of $18.3 trillion. A whopping 80 percent increase!

Of all the items in the US budget, annual interest on the national debt must be paid in full before one dime can be spent on any other budget item—defense, welfare, pensions, or anything else.

TABLE 2.16. National debt, debt interest, budget deficits, spending, and revenue, 1976–1985

CBO Budget Data	1976	1977	1978	1979	1980	1981	1982	1983	1984	1985
Revenues	$298	$356	$400	$463	$517	$599	$618	$601	$666	$734
Debt Interest	$27	$30	$36	$43	$53	$69	$85	$90	$111	$130
Total Spending	$372	$409	$459	$504	$591	$678	$746	$808	$852	$946
Federal Deficit	$74	$54	$59	$41	$74	$79	$128	$208	$185	$212
Gross Public Debt (Nat Debt)	$629	$706	$777	$830	$909	$995	$1,137	$1,372	$1,565	$1,817
Deficit as Pct. of Spending	19.82%	13.12%	12.91%	8.08%	12.49%	11.65%	17.17%	25.71%	21.77%	22.43%
Deficit as Pct of Revenues	24.72%	15.11%	14.82%	8.78%	14.27%	13.18%	20.72%	34.60%	27.82%	28.92%
Deficit as Pct. of Nat. Debt	11.72%	7.60%	7.62%	4.91%	8.12%	7.94%	11.25%	15.15%	11.85%	11.68%
Deficit as Pct of GDP	3.89%	2.69%	2.69%	1.63%	2.64%	2.47%	3.66%	5.62%	4.64%	5.05%
Debt Int. as Pct. of Spending	7.18%	7.31%	7.74%	8.45%	8.88%	10.14%	11.40%	11.11%	13.04%	13.68%
Debt Int. as Pct of Revenues	8.96%	8.41%	8.89%	9.19%	10.15%	11.48%	13.76%	14.95%	16.67%	17.64%
Debt Int. as Pct of Nat. Debt	4.24%	4.23%	4.57%	5.14%	5.78%	6.92%	7.47%	6.55%	7.10%	7.13%
Debt Int. as Pct. of GDP	1.41%	1.50%	1.61%	1.70%	1.88%	2.15%	2.43%	2.43%	2.78%	3.08%
GDP	$1,900	$2,000	$2,200	$2,500	$2,800	$3,200	$3,500	$3,700	$4,000	$4,200
Nat. Debt as Pct of GDP	33.11%	35.32%	35.30%	33.18%	32.48%	31.09%	32.49%	37.07%	39.12%	43.27%
In Billions										

Note: the average national debt-to-GDP ratio for this ten-year period was 35.2 percent. The average national debt was $1.02 trillion, and average total spending per year was $635 billion. The interest paid on the national debt over this period averaged 5.91 percent.

TABLE 2.17. National debt, debt interest, budget deficits, spending, and revenue, 2009–2018

CBO Budget Data

	2009	2010	2011	2012	2013	2014	2015	2016	2017	2018
Revenues	2585.8	2298.1	2314.8	2305.8	2596	3083.6	3331.7	3561.4	3750.6	3973.9
Debt Interest at 3% Avg Int Rate	142.7	135.9	254.5	348.8	222.8	222.9	253.6	300.1	373.4	461.5
Total Spending	3997.8	3591.1	3614.8	3632.8	3685	3777.8	3908.2	4089.8	4247.5	4449.2
Federal Deficit	1412	1298	1300	1327	1089	744.2	576.5	528.4	486.9	475.3
Gross Public Debt (Nat Debt)	12867.5	14456.3	15673.9	16566.7	17249.3	18046.9	19147.8	20006.6	20876.5	21696.2
Deficit as Pct. of Spending	35.32%	36.01%	35.96%	36.53%	29.55%	19.70%	14.75%	12.92%	11.46%	10.68%
Deficit as Pct of Revenues	54.61%	56.26%	56.16%	57.55%	41.95%	24.13%	17.30%	14.84%	12.95%	11.96%
Deficit as Pct of Nat. Debt	10.97%	8.94%	8.29%	8.01%	6.31%	4.08%	3.01%	2.64%	2.33%	2.19%
Deficit as Pct of GDP	10.09%	8.98%	8.55%	8.45%	6.72%	4.46%	3.37%	3.00%	2.70%	2.56%
Debt Int. as Pct. of Spending	3.57%	3.78%	7.04%	9.60%	6.05%	5.90%	6.49%	7.34%	8.79%	10.37%
Debt Int. as Pct of Revenues	5.52%	5.91%	10.99%	15.13%	8.58%	7.35%	7.61%	8.43%	9.93%	11.61%
Debt Int. as Pct of Nat. Debt	1.11%	0.94%	1.62%	2.11%	1.29%	1.22%	1.32%	1.50%	1.79%	2.13%
Debt Int. as Pct of GDP	1.02%	0.94%	1.67%	2.22%	1.38%	1.34%	1.48%	1.71%	2.07%	2.49%
GDP	$14,000	$14,400	$15,200	$15,700	$16,200	$16,676	$17,126	$17,589	$18,064	$18,551
Nat. Debt as Pct of GDP	91.91%	100.39%	103.12%	105.51%	106.48%	109.42%	111.80%	113.86%	115.57%	116.95%

Note: the average national debt-to-GDP ratio for this ten-year period between 2009 and 2018 was 107.5 percent. The average national debt was $17.68 trillion, and the average total spending per year was $3.899 trillion. All budget figures after 2013 are estimated and were posted on the government's web page.

The national debt will be severely affected by interest rate increases. Unless matching revenue increases or budget cuts offset rate increases, the increased interest amounts will result in increased budget deficits and raise the national debt even more, which in turn will result in even-higher budget deficits and a higher national debt, and so on. If it seems like this is a problem spiraling out of control, then you understand one of the points I'm trying to convey. It's the equivalent of having a credit card with an unlimited line. Uncle Sam uses the national debt to pay its bills and to pay the interest on the money it has borrowed. We have a government that fiscally is totally out of control. It puts many costly programs into effect, borrows from the national debt to fund them, and lets the next administration worry about getting expenses under control.

Not Just Possible But Probable

As they have been asking on the financial newscasts, what happens when the Fed pulls away the punch bowl? In my opinion, the Fed's power to control interest rates is strong, but the Fed is far from invincible. It pushed interest rates down to record lows, but it had to purchase $85 billion a month in debt securities to keep it down. The mere hint that the low-rate era is coming to an end caused a major disruption in bond markets in July 2013. Interest rates on the ten-year treasury jumped 50 percent, from 1.8 percent to 2.7 percent, in just a few days. This was in spite of the fact that the Fed made no change in its rate policy. In my opinion, without the Fed's support, interest rates would be substantially higher.

In order to show the effect a return to a normal rate would have on the national debt, I created two tables. Table 2.18 shows what would happen if the average rate returned to 4 percent, followed by table 2.19, showing what would happen at a 6 percent average rate. I believe 6 percent is closer to where rates would be if the Fed allowed them to float freely. Each table assumes annual budget deficits of $600 billion and, by extension, annual national-debt increases of the same amount.

Note that one year after rates hit 4 percent, the debt interest jumps to $604 billion and, by year three, to $700 billion. That amounts to increases of $381 billion and $478 billion, respectively. At the 6 percent rate, the figures are substantially higher. After one year, debt interest would jump to $757 billion and, after three years, to $974 billion, which equates to increases of $534 billion and $742 billion, respectively. How likely is it that Congress and the president could come up with $500–$700 billion in spending cuts or tax increases to offset the increased budget requirements needed to fund the debt? I think "slim to none" is the appropriate answer.

TABLE 2.18. Hypothetical 2013–2023 financial data assuming interest rates of 4 percent and budget deficits of $600 billion

CBO Budget Data

	2013	2014	2015	2016	2017	2018	2019	2020	2021	2022	2023
Revenues	$2,596.0	$3,177.8	$3,308.2	$3,489.8	$3,647.5	$3,849.2	$4,093.1	$4,215.9	$4,342.4	$4,472.7	$4,606.8
Debt Interest at 4% Avg Int Rate*	$222.8	$604.2	$632.5	$700.8	$715.0	$769.2	$798.7	$828.1	$854.5	$881.0	$907.6
Total Spending	$3,685.0	$3,777.8	$3,908.2	$4,089.8	$4,247.5	$4,449.2	$4,582.7	$4,720.2	$4,861.8	$5,007.6	$5,157.8
Federal Deficit**	$1,089.0	$600.0	$600.0	$600.0	$600.0	$600.0	$600.0	$600.0	$600.0	$600.0	$600.0
Gross Public Debt (Nat Debt)	$17,249.3	$18,248.9	$19,147.8	$20,026.6	$20,876.5	$21,696.2	$22,347.1	$23,017.5	$23,708.0	$24,419.3	$25,151.8
Deficit as Pct of Spending	29.55%	15.88%	15.35%	14.67%	14.13%	13.49%	13.09%	12.71%	12.34%	11.98%	11.63%
Deficit as Pct of Revenues	41.95%	18.88%	18.14%	17.19%	16.45%	15.59%	14.66%	14.23%	13.82%	13.41%	13.02%
Deficit as Pct of Nat Debt	6.31%	3.29%	3.13%	3.00%	2.87%	2.77%	2.68%	2.61%	2.53%	2.46%	2.39%
Deficit as Pct of GDP	6.72%	3.60%	3.50%	3.41%	3.32%	3.23%	3.14%	3.05%	2.96%	2.87%	2.79%
Debt Int as Pct of Spending	6.05%	15.99%	16.70%	17.14%	17.31%	17.29%	17.43%	17.54%	17.58%	17.59%	17.60%
Debt Int as Pct of Revenues	8.58%	19.01%	19.72%	20.08%	20.15%	19.98%	19.51%	19.64%	19.68%	19.70%	19.70%
Debt Int as Pct of Nat Debt	1.29%	3.31%	3.41%	3.50%	3.52%	3.55%	3.57%	3.60%	3.60%	3.61%	3.61%
Debt Int as Pct of GDP	1.38%	3.62%	3.81%	3.98%	4.07%	4.15%	4.18%	4.21%	4.22%	4.22%	4.22%
GDP	$16,200	$16,676	$17,126	$17,589	$18,064	$18,551	$19,108	$19,681	$20,272	$20,880	$21,506
Nat. Debt as Pct of GDP	106.48%	109.42%	111.80%	113.86%	115.57%	116.95%	116.95%	116.95%	116.95%	116.95%	116.95%

Note: The years 2019 through 2025 assume 3 percent annual growth. The debt-interest amount of 4 percent was taken directly from table 2.9, "National Debt Interest with $600 Billion Annual Deficits." This table assumes the Federal Reserve raised the average interest rate from 3 percent to 4 percent.

TABLE 2.19. Hypothetical 2013–2023 financial data assuming interest rates of 6 percent and budget deficits of $600 billion

CBO Budget Data

	2013	2014	2015	2016	2017	2018	2019	2020	2021	2022	2023
Revenues	$2,596	$3,178	$3,308	$3,490	$3,648	$3,849	$4,093	$4,216	$4,342	$4,473	$4,607
Debt Interest at 6% Avg Int Rate	$223	$757	$866	$974	$1,041	$1,108	$1,180	$1,212	$1,255	$1,299	$1,343
Total Spending	$3,685	$3,778	$3,908	$4,090	$4,248	$4,449	$4,583	$4,720	$4,862	$5,008	$5,158
Federal Deficit	$1,089	$600	$600	$600	$600	$600	$600	$600	$600	$600	$600
Gross Public Debt (Nat Debt)	$17,249	$18,247	$19,148	$20,027	$20,877	$21,696	$22,347	$23,017	$23,708	$24,419	$25,152
Deficit as Pct of Spending	29.55%	15.88%	15.35%	14.67%	14.13%	13.49%	13.09%	12.71%	12.34%	11.98%	11.63%
Deficit as Pct of Revenues	41.95%	18.88%	18.14%	17.19%	16.45%	15.59%	14.66%	14.23%	13.82%	13.41%	13.02%
Deficit as Pct of Nat Debt	6.31%	3.29%	3.13%	3.00%	2.87%	2.77%	2.68%	2.61%	2.53%	2.46%	2.39%
Deficit as Pct of GDP	6.72%	3.60%	3.50%	3.41%	3.32%	3.23%	3.14%	3.05%	2.96%	2.87%	2.79%
Debt Int as Pct of Spending	6.05%	15.99%	16.70%	17.14%	17.31%	17.29%	17.43%	17.54%	17.58%	17.59%	17.80%
Debt Int as Pct of Revenues	8.58%	19.01%	19.72%	20.08%	20.15%	19.98%	19.51%	19.64%	19.68%	19.70%	19.70%
Debt Int as Pct of Nat Debt	1.29%	3.31%	3.41%	3.50%	3.52%	3.55%	3.57%	3.60%	3.60%	3.61%	3.61%
Debt Int as Pct of GDP	1.38%	3.62%	3.81%	3.98%	4.07%	4.15%	4.18%	4.21%	4.22%	4.22%	4.22%
GDP	$16,200	$16,676	$17,126	$17,589	$18,064	$18,551	$19,108	$19,681	$20,272	$20,880	$21,506
Nat. Debt as Pct of GDP	106.48%	109.42%	111.80%	113.98%	115.57%	116.95%	116.95%	116.95%	116.95%	118.95%	116.95%

Note: The years 2019 through 2025 assume 3 percent annual growth. The debt-interest amount of 6 percent was taken directly from the table 2.9, "National-Debt Interest with $600 Billion

Annual Deficits." The data assumes the Federal Reserve raised
the average interest rate from 3 percent to 6 percent.

I previously stated that I viewed 6 percent as the most likely rate over
the long term, as that was the closest to the average of the last four decades.
If the scenario for this figure should play out as predicted, within four
years of the rate increase, debt-interest payments would exceed $1 trillion
annually and would increase by $60 billion or more every year after that. If
the government were to dump the trillion-dollar deficit into the national
debt, that all by itself would add $60 billion in debt interest. Add to that
the debt interest resulting from budget overruns, and we are talking about
maybe another $30–$40 billion. This is the scenario I see as most likely to
play out.

Is the Fed Locked In to Low Interest Rates?

The Federal Reserve is supposed to be independent of any political influence. The position of chairperson of the Fed passed from Ben Bernanke to
Dr. Janet Yellen in early 2014. It is impossible to predict when the Fed will
pull away the punch bowl, but it is possible this will not happen during the
Obama presidency. I think it's likely that the president will put pressure on
the Federal Reserve chairperson to keep rates as low as possible.

The potential economic chaos that rate increases will cause is a major
incentive for the Federal Reserve to keep rates lower than economic conditions would warrant, placing additional risk on our economy. Increasing
rates will slow the economy, raise unemployment, and reflect negatively
on Presidents Obama's legacy. Can the Fed still effectively fight inflation?
Yes, it can, but at a much higher cost to taxpayers because of the rapid
growth in the national debt.

The president's concern is well justified. A return to a 6 percent rate
and the need to find ways to deal with an additional $500–$700 billion in
budget shortfalls would cause major fiscal and political disruptions. That
reduction of that amount of money would be a direct hit to the US economy. It would increase the size of the national budget by 10–15 percent all

by itself. As I previously stated, it is unlikely that our political leadership will properly address the problem; it's more likely it will just push the deficits into the national debt.

The 1 Percent Factor, Part Two

Tables 2.20 and 2.21 show the effect of each 1 percent interest rate change on debt-interest expense for both our current $18 trillion national debt and for a future $20 trillion national debt.

TABLE 2.20. Interest on an $18 trillion national debt (in 1 percent increments)

National Debt	Interest Rate	Amount of National Debt Subject to Rate Increase	After 1 Year	After 2 Years	After 3 years	After 4 years	After 5 years	After 10 Years
$18,000	1%	$180	$74	$100	$125	$137	$147	$166.55
$18,000	2%	$360	$149	$200	$272	$273	$295	$333.72
$18,000	3%	$540	$223	$300	$377	$410	$442	$500.53
$18,000	4%	$720	$297	$400	$503	$545	$590	$667.44
$18,000	5%	$900	$372	$500	$629	$683	$737	$834.30
$18,000	6%	$1,080	$445	$600	$755	$820	$885	$1,001.16
$18,000	7%	$1,260	$520	$701	$881	$956	$1,032	$1,168.02
$18,000	8%	$1,440	$595	$801	$1,007	$1,093	$1,179	$1,334.88
$18,000	9%	$1,620	$669	$901	$1,132	$1,230	$1,327	$1,501.74
$18,000	10%	$1,800	$743	$1,001	$1,228	$1,366	$1,474	$1,668.60
$18,000	11%	$1,980	$818	$1,101	$1,384	$1,503	$1,622	$1,835.46
$18,000	12%	$2,160	$892	$1,201	$1,510	$1,639	$1,769	$2,002.32
$18,000	13%	$2,340	$965	$1,301	$1,636	$1,776	$1,916	$2,169.18

In Billions
Percent of debt subject to new rate: 41.30% | 55.60% | 69.90% | 75.90% | 81.90% | 92.70%

TABLE 2.21. Interest on a $20 trillion national debt (in 1 percent increments)

National Debt	Interest Rate	Amount of Nat'l Debt Subject to Rate Increase	After 1 Year	After 2 Years	After 3 Years	After 4 Years	After 5 Years	After 10 Years
$20,000	1%	$200	$83	$111	$140	$152	$164	185.4
$20,000	2%	$400	$165	$222	$280	$304	$328	370.8
$20,000	3%	$600	$248	$334	$419	$455	$491	556.2
$20,000	4%	$800	$330	$445	$559	$607	$655	741.6
$20,000	5%	$1,000	$413	$556	$699	$759	$819	927
$20,000	6%	$1,200	$496	$667	$839	$911	$983	1112.4
$20,000	7%	$1,400	$578	$778	$979	$1,063	$1,147	1297.8
$20,000	8%	$1,600	$661	$890	$1,118	$1,214	$1,310	1483.2
$20,000	9%	$1,800	$743	$1,001	$1,258	$1,366	$1,474	1668.6
$20,000	10%	$2,000	$826	$1,112	$1,398	$1,518	$1,638	1854
$20,000	11%	$2,200	$909	$1,223	$1,538	$1,670	$1,802	2039.4
$20,000	12%	$2,400	$991	$1,334	$1,678	$1,822	$1,966	2224.8
$20,000	13%	$2,600	$1,074	$1,446	$1,817	$1,973	$2,129	2410.2

In Billions
Percent of debt subject to the new rate: 41.30% | 55.60% | 69.90% | 75.90% | 81.90% | 92.70%

In 1978, the Federal Reserve gained the responsibility of seeking full employment in addition to fulfilling its existing mandate of fighting inflation with the implementation of the Full Employment and Balanced Growth Act. It appears to me that these two mandates are in direct conflict. Should the Fed need to raise interest rates to battle inflation, it would slow the economy and simultaneously increase unemployment.

Interest rates have been so low for so long that it is easy to forget what normal rates are. The Fed's low-interest rate policy since the start of the 2008 recession, along with the Obama administration's effort to diminish this issue, has effectively taken the seriousness of the national debt problem out of the public eye. At the present time, the Fed's ability to push down interest rates in spite of this country's declining creditworthiness remains unchallenged. It is the size of the US economy, not its strength, that allows the Fed this flexibility.

The ramifications of the ever-increasing national debt will eventually overwhelm our budgets. There is little doubt the Fed is losing its ability to control interest rates. It's not a matter of if but when! Look at Greece, Italy, and Spain as examples of countries with out-of-control spending and huge debt problems that could not be controlled by their central banks.

The fact that investors throughout the world are willing to commit to lending our country trillions of dollars for ten years or longer at an interest rate below 3 or 4 percent is mind-boggling. When our country 'fesses up to the problem, it will probably not be by choice but because of some fiscal crisis. The actions the government needs to take now to address the problem will cause major pain in all parts of the economy, and the amount of pain will increase in proportion to the growth of the national debt. As the saying goes, "Pay me now, or pay me later"—but sometimes the debt must be paid. With the return to normal interest rates and the ever-growing national debt, I predict that within five years after the Federal Reserve normalizes rates, debt interest will cost taxpayers $1 trillion a year and keep growing. When taxpayers realize that at least twenty cents out of every tax dollar collected will go toward funding the debt and not toward providing any benefits to anyone, they might wake up to the problem. As of now, very few people truly understand the problem—not even most politicians and educators.

In addition to the concerns I just stated, there is the possibility that normal interest rates would be a little higher than they were over the last four decades. The ballooning national debt and severely unbalanced budgets have caused Standard & Poor's (S&P) to downgrade US debt, and the other major rating agencies are contemplating similar action.

Will Prosperity Heal the Problem?

All through this write-up, I've been beating the drum on the severity of the national-debt problem, the general population's ignorance of the subject, and our leadership's deliberate misinformation. The most common argument politicians use in defense of the national debt is that the problem can be eliminated through economic growth. Proving or disproving this is difficult, but I'll give it a try.

The growth argument infers government revenues will grow faster than government spending and that sustained growth will be large enough to eliminate budget deficits, negating the need to increase the national debt. A review of the growth of the national debt over the last decade shows the absurdity of that argument.

I started by making the assumption that the best method for measuring the likelihood of growth in national tax revenues is to compare it to GDP growth. Since the GDP is the best indicator of growth or recession, it is also the most comprehensive measurement of money moving through the economy. Logically, larger growth in GDP should equate to larger growth in tax revenues.

In order to determine the relationship between GDP growth and tax revenue growth, I looked at both of these figures for every year from 1967 through 2013. This is not a very scientific process and does not account for any revenues resulting from new taxes levied by Congress, but I think it may provide some meaningful results.

The best way to explain the process I used in determining revenue growth is to cite an example. Table 2.22 shows that in 2010, the government took in $2.162 trillion in revenues and the nation's GDP grew at 3.02

percent. Revenues that year grew by $57 billion from the previous year and grew an additional $141 billion the following year. Using this data, I grouped together all the years with the same GDP growth and averaged them. Then I grouped together and averaged all the years where GDP grew between 2 and 3 percent. In addition, for each year I took the average of the year's growth (in this example, $57 billion) and the following year's growth of $141 billion and averaged the two-year total. (In this example, the two-year average would be $99 billion.)

TABLE 2.22. Revenues and GDP figures, 1967–2013

Year	Amt rev's incr. or decr. in the next year in dollars	Amt rev's incr. or decr. in the next year in percent	Total revenues collected	GDP growth		Year	Amt rev's incr. or decr. in the next year in dollars	Amt rev's incr. or decr. in the next year in percent	Total revenues collected	GDP growth
2013			$2,712							
2012	$262	10.69%	$2,450	2.20%	***	1989	$41	4.14%	$991	3.53%
2011	$147	6.38%	$2,303	1.70%	***	1988	$82	9.02%	$909	4.12%
2010	$141	6.52%	$2,162	3.02%	***	1987	$55	6.44%	$854	3.34%
2009	$57	2.71%	$2,105	-3.53%	***	1986	$85	11.05%	$769	3.43%
2008	-$419	-16.60%	$2,524	-0.36%	***	1985	$35	4.77%	$734	4.10%
2007	-$44	-1.71%	$2,568	1.91%	***	1984	$68	10.21%	$666	7.20%
2006	$273	11.34%	$2,407	2.66%	***	1983	$66	11.00%	$600	4.52%
2005	$254	11.80%	$2,153	3.08%	***	1982	-$18	-2.91%	$618	-1.97%
2004	$273	14.52%	$1,880	3.48%	***	1981	$19	3.17%	$599	2.52%
2003	$88	4.91%	$1,792	2.55%	***	1980	$82	15.86%	$517	-0.24%
2002	-$61	-3.29%	$1,853	1.83%	***	1979	$54	11.66%	$463	3.18%
2001	-$138	-6.93%	$1,991	1.09%	***	1978	$63	15.75%	$400	5.62%
2000	-$34	-1.68%	$2,025	4.17%	***	1977	$44	12.36%	$356	4.66%
1999	$198	10.84%	$1,827	4.49%	***	1976	$58	19.46%	$298	5.38%
1998	$105	6.10%	$1,722	4.22%	***	1975	$19	6.81%	$279	-0.18%
1997	$143	9.06%	$1,579	4.55%	***	1974	$16	6.08%	$263	-0.47%
1996	$126	8.67%	$1,453	3.75%	***	1973	$32	13.85%	$231	5.88%
1995	$102	7.55%	$1,351	2.54%	***	1972	$24	11.59%	$207	5.59%
1994	$93	7.39%	$1,258	4.06%	***	1971	$20	10.70%	$187	3.46%
1993	$104	9.01%	$1,154	2.69%	***	1970	-$6	-3.11%	$193	0.00%
1992	$63	5.77%	$1,091	3.34%	***	1969	$6	3.21%	$187	2.67%
1991	$36	3.41%	$1,055	-0.19%	***	1968	$34	22.22%	$153	4.19%
1990	$23	2.23%	$1,032	1.86%	***	1967	$4	2.68%	$149	2.72%

In billions

Note: The figures in these tables are taken from US budget figures based on a fiscal year that starts on October 1. The GDP growth figures are based on the normal calendar year.

The Fed may not take action on interest rates for a long time, but when it does it will probably be because the growth rate has reached the targets it set or because inflation has become a problem and has to be tamed. The question that has to be answered is, if the Fed returns to normal interest rates, will the growth in GDP have generated enough revenue to offset the increased debt interest on the national debt? In 2012 the average interest rate paid on the national debt was 2.1 percent. Let's say the Fed raises the average rate from between 2 to 4 percent to between 4 and 6 percent. To offset rate increases on a $17 trillion national debt would require the revenues shown in table 2.23.

TABLE 2.23. Percentage of debt interest subject to the increased rate

		4%	5%	6%
First year	41.30%	$140	$211	$281
Second year	55.60%	$189	$284	$378
Third year	69.90%	$238	$356	$475
Fifth year	81.90%	$278	$418	$557
Tenth year	92.70%	$315	$473	$630

Note: Figures in billions.

TABLE 2.24. Revenue growth compared to GDP growth, 1967–2013

GDP for the year	Amount revenues increased or decreased in the following year from the current year.	Amount revenues increased or decreased from the previous year to the current year.	Year	Total revenues collected	Revenue growth for the 2 year period	Average per year	Growth rate as compared to the current years revenues.	GDP growth rate category	Total growth of all years in category	Average for each year in category
		$282	2013	2712						
-3.53%	$57	-$419	2009	2105	-$362	-181	-8.60%	Over 1% Neg Growth		
-1.97%	-$18	$19	1982	618	$1	1	0.08%	Over 1% Neg Growth	-8.52%	-4.28%
-0.47%	$16	$32	1974	263	$48	24	9.13%	0% to 1% Neg Growth		
-0.36%	-$419	-$44	2008	2524	-$463	-232	-9.17%	0% to 1% Neg Growth		
-0.24%	$82	$54	1980	517	$136	68	13.15%	0% to 1% Neg Growth		
-0.19%	$36	$23	1991	1055	$99	30	2.80%	0% to 1% Neg Growth		
-0.18%	$19	$16	1975	279	$35	18	6.27%	0% to 1% Neg Growth		
0.00%	-$6	$6	1970	198	$0	0	0.00%	0% to 1% Neg Growth	22.17%	3.70%
1.09%	-$138	-$34	2001	1991	-$172	-86	-4.32%	1% to 2% growth		
1.70%	$147	$141	2011	2308	$288	144	6.25%	1% to 2% growth		
1.83%	-$61	-$138	2002	1853	-$199	-100	-5.37%	1% to 2% growth		
1.86%	$23	$41	1990	1032	$64	32	3.10%	1% to 2% growth		
1.91%	-$44	$161	2007	2568	$117	59	2.28%	1% to 2% growth	19.4%	0.39%
2.20%	$262	$147	2012	2450	$409	205	8.35%	2% to 3% growth		
2.52%	$19	$82	1981	599	$101	51	8.43%	2% to 3% growth		
2.54%	$102	$93	1995	1351	$195	98	7.22%	2% to 3% growth		
2.55%	$88	-$61	2003	1792	$27	14	0.75%	2% to 3% growth		
2.68%	$161	$254	2006	2407	$415	208	8.62%	2% to 3% growth		
2.67%	$6	$34	1969	187	$40	20	10.70%	2% to 3% growth		
2.69%	$104	$63	1993	1154	$167	84	7.24%	2% to 3% growth		
2.72%	$4	$149	1967	149	$153	77	51.34%	2% to 3% growth	102.64%	12.83%
3.02%	$141	$57	2010	2162	$198	99	4.58%	3% to 4% growth		
3.09%	$254	$273	2005	2153	$527	264	12.24%	3% to 4% growth		
3.18%	$54	$63	1979	463	$117	59	12.65%	3% to 4% growth		
3.34%	$63	$36	1992	1091	$99	50	4.54%	3% to 4% growth		
3.34%	$55	$85	1987	854	$140	70	8.20%	3% to 4% growth		
3.43%	$85	$35	1986	769	$120	60	7.80%	3% to 4% growth		
3.46%	$20	-$6	1971	187	$14	7	3.74%	3% to 4% growth		
3.48%	$273	$88	2004	1880	$361	181	9.60%	3% to 4% growth		
3.53%	$41	$82	1989	991	$123	62	6.21%	3% to 4% growth		
3.75%	$126	$102	1996	1453	$228	114	7.85%	3% to 4% growth	77.39%	7.74%
4.06%	$95	$104	1994	1258	$197	99	7.83%	4% to 5% Growth		
4.10%	$35	$68	1985	734	$103	52	7.02%	4% to 5% Growth		
4.12%	$82	$55	1988	908	$137	69	7.54%	4% to 5% Growth		
4.17%	-$34	$198	2000	2025	$164	82	4.05%	4% to 5% Growth		
4.19%	$34	$4	1968	153	$38	19	12.42%	4% to 5% Growth		
4.22%	$105	$143	1998	1722	$248	124	7.20%	4% to 5% Growth		
4.49%	$198	$105	1999	1827	$303	152	8.29%	4% to 5% Growth		
4.52%	$66	-$18	1983	600	$48	24	4.00%	4% to 5% Growth		
4.55%	$143	$126	1997	1579	$269	135	8.52%	4% to 5% Growth		
4.66%	$44	$58	1977	356	$102	51	14.33%	4% to 5% Growth	81.19%	8.12%
5.38%	$58	$19	1976	298	$77	39	12.92%	5% to 6% growth		
5.59%	$24	$20	1972	207	$44	22	10.63%	5% to 6% growth		
5.62%	$63	$44	1978	400	$107	54	13.38%	5% to 6% growth		
5.88%	$32	$24	1973	231	$56	28	12.12%	5% to 6% growth	49.04%	12.26%
7.20%	$68	$66	1984	666	$134	67	10.06%	over 6% growth	10.06%	10.06%

In normal times, the interest rate needed to fund the national debt would be in the 5–6 percent range. Table 2.25 illustrates how much tax revenues would have to grow in order to offset the increased debt interest resulting from rate increases. The table shows that if the Fed were to raise interest rates to 5 percent, tax revenues would have to grow by 7.7 percent in the first year and 13.1 percent by the third year. A rate rise to 6 percent would require revenue growth of 10.3 percent in the first year and 17.5 percent by the third year.

TABLE 2.25. Revenue growth needed to offset interest-expense increases resulting from Fed rate hikes

	Percent of debt interest subject to the increased rate	Amount of int expense added if the Fed increased rates to 5%	Percent revenues needed to grow to offset added interest expense	Amount of interest expense added if the Fed increased rates to 6%	Percent revenues needed to grow to offset added interest expense
First Year	41.30%	$211	7.77%	$281	10.36%
Second Year	55.60%	$284	10.46%	$378	13.94%
Third Year	69.90%	$356	13.14%	$475	17.53%
Fifth Year	81.90%	$418	15.40%	$557	20.54%
Tenth Year	92.70%	$473	17.43%	$630	23.24%

Based on 2013 total revenues of $2,712 trillion and a national debt of $17 trillion.

Using the revenue data cited in the table, I grouped together all the years that had similar GDP growth in table 2.26 to gauge how and if it also resulted in revenue growth. For example, I grouped together all the years that had GDP growth between 2 and 3 percent and compared them to the years that had GDP growth between 3 and 4 percent to determine if revenue growth increased proportionally to GDP growth.

TABLE 2.26. Revenue growth in relation to GDP growth

Group name	GDP growth rate	Number of years in sample	Average increase in revenue growth	Amount of increased revenue growth if applied to 2013 revenue figure of $2,712 trillion
A	Over 1% neg growth	2	-4.26%	-$115.50
B	-1% to 0%	6	3.70%	$100.23
C	1% to 2%	5	0.39%	$10.54
D	2% to 3%	8	12.83%	$347.96
E	3% to 4%	10	7.74%	$209.87
F	4% to 5%	10	8.12%	$220.18
G	5% to 6%	4	12.26%	$332.52
Totals		45	7.24%	$196.38

Note - A minimum sample of 2 years is required

51

Does GDP Growth Translate into Revenue Growth?

Obviously GDP growth does result in revenue growth. Unfortunately it is nowhere near enough to offset the increased interest expense on the national debt with rates at 5 or 6 percent. The following is a list of some conclusions we can draw from this analysis:

1. There is no direct link between GDP growth and revenue growth. In fact, of the four groups shown in table 2.26 (D–G), the one with the lowest average GDP growth had the highest growth in revenues.

2. The amount of revenue growth varies widely even when the GDP growth rate is constant. For example, in group F there were ten sample years where GDP growth averaged between 4 and 5 percent, yet within that group, revenue increases were as low as 4 percent and as high as 14 percent.

3. Over the forty-five-year sample period, revenue growth averaged 7.24 percent. This equates to a $196 billion increase in 2013 revenues. Only 41 percent of any rate increase is affected in year one. The $196 billion increase will not even cover that and will cover only about 50 percent of the increase payable in year three. Review the revenue increases needed to offset a 5 or 6 percent interest rate in table 2.25 to determine the probable shortfall.

There are other concerns associated with this issue as well. There is no guarantee that revenue increases gained through GDP growth will be used to offset increased interest expense. It is more likely that the president and Congress will want to use the revenue to fund new projects or to help foster their political agendas.

The government counts all Social Security income it receives as part of the total revenues. In 1967, it amounted to 22 percent of revenues. By 2013, that figure climbed to 35 percent. I cannot speak to the issue of how the government will meet its Social Security obligations in the future.

When Will Our Leaders Deal with the Problem?

Looking to GDP growth as a cure for our national-debt problem is foolish and unrealistic. This analysis of the national debt does not cover every aspect of the issue, but it does make clear that our country has a serious problem.

It is clear that growing our way out of the problem is not the answer. I must be delusional in thinking that I identified a problem that will eventually bring our country to its knees, and nobody else seems to think the problem is severe enough to bring it to the attention of the general public. In my opinion this issue shines a bright light on our leadership and shows them to be politically gutless; they avoid the issue in order not to jeopardize their own reelection chances, for fear of being exposed as unworthy of the offices they hold because they are incapable of understanding an issue on which they are supposed to take the lead. We have an uninformed voting public as a result of incompetent leadership.

The heads of the Federal Reserve, Ben Bernanke and later Janet Yellen, should be pounding the table on this issue. Instead they defer to Congress and the president because they use the excuse that these are political issues, and taxing is out of the jurisdiction of the Federal Reserve. Their job is to fight inflation and help employment, so they say. The national debt issue has a major impact on both.

The way things look now, the budget deficits will continue and the national debt will continue to balloon. Therefore, we can assume that the problem, as bad as it is, will continue to worsen. We cannot grow our way out of this problem. It will require major spending cuts and tax increases. We already know those are not going to happen.

My goal here is to alert you to the potential damage our country faces as a result of this problem. I'm neither an economist nor a mathematician, and there are probably many mathematical booboos and some assumptions that are off base in this book. Nevertheless, any errors that do exist should not detract from the message. I'm in way over my head on this subject, and I left plenty of unanswered questions, but there were some things I felt had to be said.

Former fed chairman Bernanke said in the past that he was comfortable with using an "exit strategy" (pushing rates back up to normal levels without creating turmoil in the financial markets), though I have yet to see it explained. In his public statements, he gives the impression that he has the situation well in hand. This begs the question: Who am I to doubt the strategy of one of the most highly respected economists on the planet?

Chapter 3: A Countdown to Detonation of the National Debt Bomb

Self-Destruction: The Facts That Prove the Theory

Communism failed to diminish the greatness of the United States. Our freedoms and capitalist system stand tall for the entire world to envy. Religious fanatics are now trying to do what communism couldn't. They too have no chance of success.

There are many countries that relish the idea of a diminished United States; however, all they have to do is wait! We are doing, and will continue to do, more damage to ourselves with the national debt crisis than most people could possibly imagine.

The national debt is a growing bubble that, in my opinion, will burst within a decade after the Federal Reserve returns rates to normal. Remember when the housing bubble burst in 2008 and all the damage it did to the US economy? We'll look back on that as a minor bump in the road when compared to the economic Armageddon that will result from the coming national-debt crisis. The following countdown to the national-debt explosion explains how we got to where we are and where we're headed.

As you know, one of the primary functions of the Federal Reserve is to set interest rates at levels that will best suit the country's economic needs. The Fed likes to have it both ways when it comes to interest rate policy. It claims it will keep the public informed on when interest rate changes are likely to take place, yet it refuses to commit to a fixed date, claiming that rate changes are data sensitive and subject to changing economic conditions. While this policy makes sense, it has resulted in what seems like a never-ending series of delays in projected rate-change moves, because the economy continues to underperform the Fed's expectations. (Over the last six years, the growth in the economy has averaged less than 2 percent annually). In early 2014, when I originally composed the timeline in the following "Countdown to Armageddon" section, it was the consensus of most financial gurus that it would be early 2015 when the Fed would start normalizing rates. Now, in October 2015, it looks like the Fed will not move on rates before late 2015 at the earliest, and possibly not before early 2016. By then, we will be looking at a national debt in excess of $18.5 trillion. The countdown to Armageddon scenario that we will go on to look at now appears to be at least one year premature. This situation cannot be avoided. This national debt issue will forever remain a moving target, making it is impossible to pin down exactly when the Federal Reserve will begin moving interest rates.

Based on this timeline, I estimate the annual budget deficit to be at $730 billion by 2017. This may appear to the reader to be an overestimate, as the 2014 fiscal year ended with a budget deficit of only $483 billion. In my opinion, this low rate is just reflective of a one or two-year aberration that can be mostly attributed to the increase in capital gains tax revenues resulting from the booming stock market. I believe that it was the direct result of the extended period of super-low interest rates that forced investors out of bonds and into stocks. In any case, it's really irrelevant since I estimated the 2014 national debt at $17.75 trillion instead of the $18 trillion it actually was, and was inclusive of the $483 billion budget deficit instead of the $750 billion deficit I had forecasted. I admit this is pure speculation on my part. However, I still stand by my estimates going forward. The point I am trying to relay to the reader is that the national debt crisis will worsen and become uncontrollable because the interest needed to fund the debt will be too great a burden for taxpayers to bear, reaching at least

$1 trillion annually when the Fed is done normalizing interest rates. And that's just for starters.

Countdown to Armageddon

Let's take a year-by-year look at the evolution of the national debt problem that has led to the current crisis and the impending worsening that will happen in the years to follow.

In the early 1980s, the national debt problem began to unfold. President Ronald Reagan successfully pushed for both a massive buildup of the military complex and a massive reduction in individual tax rates. The national debt, as a percentage of GDP, jumped from about 35 percent to about 55 percent during this period. Reagan was not the first president to use deficit spending to meet budget needs, but, to the best of my knowledge, he was the first who believed it was an acceptable way of meeting a political agenda, and he made it easy for future presidents to follow suit.

1989

Average Interest Rate 8%

National Debt Amount	Budget Deficit	Debt Interest
$2,857	$161	$165

All figures in billions

Things went downhill a little further during the George H. Bush presidency. The debt-to-GDP ratio jumped an additional 10 percent, to 65 percent. One of the major reasons for this was the cost of the war with Iraq. However, the downward trend reversed a little during the Clinton presidency. The dot-com (technology) boom caused a ten-point improvement, pushing the debt-to-GDP ratio back down to 55 percent.

During the George W. Bush presidency, the national debt problem took a major turn for the worse. The Gulf War in Afghanistan and the second Iraqi war caused large increases in deficit spending. In those eight years, the budget deficit exceeded $425 billion only once, and that was in his last year in office, 2009, when it skyrocketed to $1.412 trillion—more than triple the previous year. That was the first time it breached the trillion-dollar mark.

The $700 billion Troubled Asset Relief Program (TARP), signed by President Bush in 2008, to bail out the banks during the subprime mortgage crisis made up the lion's share of that budget deficit. Almost all the TARP loans made to banks were paid back to the US Treasury. Since this $700 billion was a part of the 2009 budget deficit, the returned funds should have been used to pay down the debt. I was unable to find out what actually happened with those returned funds.

By the end of George W. Bush's presidency, the debt-to-GDP ratio had reached 80 percent. The national-debt problem was getting serious, yet there was still no concern and no pain. Politicians gave the subject some lip service and little else.

2008

Average Interest Rate 4%

National Debt Amount	Budget Deficit	Debt Interest
$10,025	$410	**$244**

President Obama adopted the trillion-dollar budget deficit threshold reached in 2009 as the standard and accumulated more than $5 trillion in budget deficits in his first term alone. This pushed the debt-to-GDP ratio to about 103 percent. The deficit spending problem had now reached a new level. The national-debt problem had become a crisis, but that's not what President Obama wants to talk about. The president and his supporters continue to lowball the problem, keeping it out of the public eye. As a result, the public continues to believe that this high level of deficit spending and $16 trillion national debt is not a serious problem.

The raging stock market, a totally distorted employment picture, and a misrepresentation of the economic growth picture support the president's position of denial. The Congressional Budget Office (CBO) was estimating an average budget deficit of $630 billion a year for the ten years that followed. Based on its past forecasts, this number is probably on the low side. The CBO has a long history of underestimating budget requirements. Its assumptions would also be subject to unforeseen economic events such as 2008's severe recession.

2012

Average Interest Rate 4%

National Debt Amount	Budget Deficit	Debt Interest
$16,066	$1,327	$225

Sometime in the next few years, the economy and unemployment will probably improve enough to meet the Federal Reserve's economic targets for returning to normal interest rates. The Fed set these targets as data points that, when reached, would show that the economy was normalizing. It is expected that the Fed will gradually reduce and eventually end its massive bond-buying program (used to keep rates down), which will be followed by a gradual increase in interest rates back to normal levels of 5 or 6 percent (from the current 2 percent). Under normal conditions, the Fed would raise rates by .025 percent each quarter, or 1 percent a year. If this happens, it will take three years to get to a 5 percent rate and four years to get to a 6 percent rate.

The political establishment and the media argue that the return to normal economic conditions will result in added revenues and reduced deficit spending. This is true, but returning to normal interest rates in response will cause more problems than it solves. It is not possible to forecast how the pain of the national-debt problem will play out as interest rates rise to normal levels, but it is clear that even though there is no pain now, there will be serious pain when normal rates return.

The financial impact on the nation's budget from the Fed's decision to return to normal rates is easily calculated; the impact on the nation's economy and its citizens is not. Determining the former is just a matter of estimating the start date and working out the numbers. I'm going on the assumption that the Fed will start raising rates in the beginning of 2015 and that rates will increase at the rate of 1 percent a year, going from 2 percent to 6 percent over a four-year period. I am assuming that no major events will alter government spending projections. I am also assuming that deficit spending will continue at a rate of $750 billion a year. If these assumptions are in the right ballpark, debt interest will jump from $355 billion in 2014 to $903 billion by 2018. Even without further interest rate increases, in the three years after that (through 2021), debt interest will jump an additional $309 billion to over $1.2 trillion. This is because existing, previously issued debt will be reissued at the higher interest rate.

In 2014, debt interest increased by only $15 billion. Interest rates remained at 2 percent. Nothing to get excited about! The only effect on the budget deficit was the additional interest expense on the previous year's budget deficit.

2014

Average Interest Rate 2%

National Debt Amount	Int. Rate on 100% of Debt	Debt Int. on 100% of Debt
$17,750	2.00%	$355

The pain associated with the Federal Reserve's program to return to normal rates is starting in 2015, with the debt interest jumping by $89 billion or 25 percent. The 1 percent rise in rates, put into effect this year, means that 40 percent of the national debt will have a 3 percent interest rate, and 60 percent will still carry a 2 percent rate. Of that $89 billion increase, $18 billion is due to the estimated $750 billion budget deficit from the previous year. From this point forward, debt interest resulting from deficit spending will not be broken out.

2015

Average Interest Rate 2%

National Debt Amount	40% of Debt at 3%	60% of Debt at 2%	Actual Debt Interest at 3%	Actual Debt Interest at 2%	Total Debt Interest
$18,500	$7,400	$11,100	$222	$222	**$444**

I predict that in 2016 the debt interest will jump by another 28 percent from the previous year, increasing $124 billion. Raising the interest rate an additional 1 percent means 40 percent of the national debt will have a 4 percent interest rate, 15 percent will have a 3 percent interest rate, and the remaining 45 percent will still carry a 2 percent rate.

2016

Average Interest Rate 4%

National Debt Amount	40% of Debt at 4%	15% of Debt at 3%	45% of Debt at 2%	Actual Debt Interest at 4%	Actual Debt Interest at 3%	Actual Debt Interest at 2%	Total Debt Interest
$19,250	$7,700	$2,888	$8,663	$308	$87	$173	$568

As of 2017, I predict that we will be into the third consecutive year of 1 percent interest rate hikes. Debt interest will jump another 28 percent from the previous year. Now 40 percent of the debt will be yielding a 5 percent rate and so on. The jump of $162 billion will bring the annual debt interest to $730 billion. Remember, just three years earlier, in 2014, the annual debt interest was $355 billion.

2017

Average Interest Rate 5%

National Debt Amount	40% of Debt at 5%	15% of Debt at 4%	15% of Debt at 3%	30% of Debt at 2%	Actual Debt Interest at 5%	Actual Debt Interest at 4%	Actual Debt Interest at 3%	Actual Debt Interest at 2%	Total Debt Interest
$20,000	$8,000	$3,000	$3,000	$6,000	$400	$120	$90	$120	$730

The last of the 1 percent rate hikes (to 6 percent) caused debt interest to jump by an additional $173 billion, or 24 percent, to $903 billion.

2018

Average Interest Rate 5%

National Debt Amount	40% of Debt at 6%	15% of Debt at 5%	15% of Debt at 4%	30% of Debt at 3% or Less	Actual Debt Interest at 6%	Actual Debt Interest at 5%	Actual Debt Interest at 4%	Actual Debt Interest at 3% or Less	Total Debt Interest
$20,750	$8,300	$3,113	$3,113	$6,225	$498	$156	$125	$125	$903

If my assumptions are correct, 2019 will be the year the annual debt interest will exceed the trillion-dollar threshold. At $1.021 trillion, the annual debt interest will be $119 billion more than the previous year—a 13 percent increase. It will grow by 13 percent even though the interest rate held steady at 6 percent for two consecutive years. The portion of the national debt subject to the 6 percent rate will go from 40 percent to 55 percent and so on.

2019

National Debt Amount	55% of Debt at 6%	15% of Debt at 5%	5% of Debt at 4%	Average Interest Rate 6%					Total Debt Interest
				25% of Debt at 3% or Less	Actual Debt Interest at 6%	Actual Debt Interest at 5%	Actual Debt Interest at 4%	Actual Debt Interest at 3% or Less	
$21,500	$11,825	$3,225	$1,075	$5,375	$710	$161	$43	$108	$1,021

In 2020, the last year in this scenario, I foresee the annual debt interest amount increasing by another $112 billion, or 9 percent, to $1.133 trillion. This will be the third year at the 6 percent rate, which will now consume 70 percent of the national debt.

For the record, if the Fed maxes out rate increases at 5 percent instead of 6 percent, the amount of debt interest over the entire period will be $156 billion less, at $977 billion.

2020

National Debt Amount	70% of Debt at 6%	5% of Debt at 5%	7% of Debt at 4%	Average Interest Rate 6%					Total Debt Interest
				18% of Debt at 3% or Less	Actual Debt Interest at 6%	Actual Debt Interest at 5%	Actual Debt Interest at 4%	Actual Debt Interest at 3% or Less	
$22,250	$15,575	$1,113	$1,558	$4,005	$935	$56	$62	$80	$1,133

Effects of Interest Rate Hikes

As I previously stated, determining the size of the national debt and the annual debt-interest payments is a relatively easy process. Determining the effect of the national-debt problem on the American way of life is a completely different matter. In this scenario, the effect of the Fed's raising rates was an additional $2.7 trillion in interest expense, meaning taxpayers would have to fork over $5.5 trillion over this seven-year period to fund the national debt.

The country is already running a $650 billion budget deficit and annual debt-interest payments of $340 billion. The interest-rate hikes will increase debt interest by $114 billion in 2015 and $793 billion by 2020, according to my projections, bringing the total debt interest to $1.13 trillion annually. These increases will have to be offset by budget cuts and tax increases or be dumped into the national debt. If you think the government will take the first option, I have a bridge to sell you.

The alternative that the government will probably adopt is to add the lion's share of debt interest to the national debt. So instead of having a $22 trillion national debt in 2020, we will be looking at a $24 trillion debt. Instead of annual debt interest of $1.13 trillion, we will have debt interest of $1.22 trillion, and that assumes a stable interest-rate environment.

The wake-up call will come in the years 2015 through 2018 as debt interest will more than double, jumping from $444 billion to $903 billion, as shown in table 3.1. The question is, Will politicians come to their senses and do what is necessary to put our economy on a sound footing or will they continue to act irresponsibly and spend to push a political agenda? The first option will require major austerity measures and inflict major pain in almost every area of the economy. The alternative scenario will bring the countdown to zero and bring on an economic Armageddon similar to what happened in Greece.

TABLE 3.1. Debt interest amounts resulting from interest-rate hikes

Year	Estimated Debt Interest	Increase from 2013	Debt Int. If Left at 2%	Pct. Increase From Prev. Yr.
2013	$340		$340	
2014	$355	$15	$355	4%
2015	$444	$104	$370	25%
2016	$568	$228	$385	28%
2017	$730	$390	$400	28%
2018	$903	$563	$415	24%
2019	$1,021	$681	$430	13%
2020	$1,133	$793	$445	10%
	$5,494	$2,774	$3,140	7 Yr. Avg. 19%

When will our leadership deal with this crisis? The Obama administration argues that the debt is manageable. In my opinion, our political leadership couldn't care less about the national debt. To them, it is just a number conservatives use to highlight excessive government spending on liberal programs. It's a thorn in their side they just wish would go away. Politicians give the debt attention only because the government is required to budget for the interest that funds it.

It will be the Federal Reserve's decision to raise interest rates, which will expose the problem and ultimately force the government to act. Unfortunately this action will also eventually cause a financial meltdown. If the government doesn't act preemptively, bondholders worldwide will deem the creditworthiness of US debt unacceptable and dump their securities on the open market. This action has the potential of causing a major spike in interest rates and will cause additional selling of both bonds and stocks, pushing interest rates to even-higher levels. This also has the potential of causing as much as a 30–50 percent drop in the stock market, or roughly five thousand to seven thousand Dow points.

Once bond traders sell the securities en masse, the Federal Reserve will be out of the picture because the free markets will overwhelm any potential Fed action. Should the Fed decide it can force rates down by buying a few trillion worth of Treasury bonds, traders worldwide will view this action as a panic move and accelerate the liquidation of their bond holdings.

The president and Congress have only two options in dealing with this problem: raising taxes and cutting spending. I'm not talking about settling normal budget differences between Democrats and Republicans; I'm talking about draconian cuts and major tax increases. If my assumptions about the depth of the forthcoming crisis are anywhere near the mark, interest rates will be pushing 7–10 percent, and debt interest will exceed $1.5 trillion annually and increase at an accelerating rate.

On the spending side, budget cutters will target government employee pensions, currently the largest expense in the budget, as well as defense, education, and welfare. Also on the list will be entitlement benefits, an issue politicians have avoided dealing with for decades. On the revenue side, there will be tax increases across the board, both individual and corporate. You can count on our resourceful political leadership to come up with a few original ideas for raising taxes. The major credit agencies' downgrades of American debt will be sure to follow and will only add fuel to the fire.

The residual effects from the financial crisis that will be incurred will reach far and wide. The country is likely to go into a severe recession. Unemployment will skyrocket; consumer confidence will tank. The government will be looking to cut expenses and raise taxes when the country's economy is in the toilet.

This crisis will cause social unrest and possible street riots. Unions will be striking or threatening to do so to demand their pension benefits back and the end to a salary freeze. Welfare recipients will be demonstrating for restoration of benefits that have been cut. The unemployed will be demonstrating for more and better jobs.

The tanking of the American economy will severely affect our European and Asian trading partners as well as every other country that has a capitalist form of government. The only winners will include Communist governments, dictatorships, and all the countries that have envied the success of our capitalist form of government and gloat in our downfall.

The political establishment will take the position that we can grow our way out of the problem. In theory this is a practical solution, but in reality it's politically impossible. The only way to stop the growth of the national debt is to balance the budget. The Obama administration was unable to balance the budget with interest rates at 2 percent (near record lows) and debt interest at only $340 billion. How in the world are coming administrations going to balance the budget when interest rates are at 5 percent or 6 percent and annual debt interest is near $1 trillion (expected by 2020)? Support for a balanced budget while the Democrats are controlling any one of the three branches of government is nil.

This scenario is pure speculation on my part. It is all but certain that the national-debt problem will not play out as described here. Predicting the chain of events leading up to a crisis is next to impossible. Nevertheless, it is safe to assume that major problems lie ahead if our leadership doesn't act. The consequences of not forcefully dealing with the current debt could be catastrophic.

In my opinion, the Obama administration bears the primary responsibility for the problem. The national debt will just about double by the end of Obama's second term. Debt interest over the entire eight years of his presidency will exceed $8 trillion. President Obama is also responsible for the party-line voting mentality that now corrupts both political parties. The vote that passed Obamacare was sixty out of sixty Democrats in favor and forty out of forty Republicans against. Here we have one hundred well-educated, allegedly smart people voting on the merits of the most important bill in many a decade, but without exception no senator broke party lines, proving that party loyalty and not the merits of the health care bill was the driving force behind its passage. I make this point to illustrate that presidential leadership on this issue, while absolutely necessary, will not be forthcoming anytime soon.

It is my opinion that our government will go on in its merry way as if the national debt were a fantasy. If leadership does this and dumps all the new debt interest from the Fed's interest rate increases into the national debt, then the worst-case scenario will come into play.

Chapter 4: Prediction: The United States Will Default on Its Debt, and the Federal Reserve Will Become Irrelevant

I cannot emphasize strongly enough the financial crisis facing our country as a result of the national debt, out-of-control spending, and budget overruns. The deeper I get into this analysis, the more certain I am that a US default is almost inevitable. Our country is on the road to financial Armageddon, and I see little hope of stopping it. The worst-case scenario is that it will end American exceptionalism in its truest form. I hope this write-up will serve as a wake-up call to all concerned Americans.

Purchasing thirty-year US Treasury bonds is a bad idea. There is a good chance you won't get all your principal back. Looking ahead to 2043, when the current thirty-year bonds mature, predicting the state of the economy, the size of the budget deficits, and the national debt is all but impossible. In my opinion, if no corrective action is taken, there is a high probability the United States will need to restructure many outstanding Treasury securities and return to investors only portions of their original investments. The consequences of such a default will be political and social Armageddon.

What actions must the government take to precipitate this crisis? The answer is none. That's right: none, because the policies that will cause a default are already in place. The government's inability to balance a budget plus the return of interest rates to normal, all by themselves, will cause this crisis. New budget-busting government programs will serve only to solidify the crisis.

If numbers could talk, the following two tables would speak volumes. Table 4.1 lists vital economic statistics for the last thirty years. Table 4.2 shows the effect of dumping the annual debt-interest payments into the national debt and how fast the debt will grow under various interest-rates scenarios. The conclusions that follow are based on the data on these two tables, as was all the analysis up to this point.

TABLE 4.1. The statistics tell the story:
The last thirty years (1984–2013)

Year	GDP Growth Rate	Annual GDP	Inflation Rate	Budget Deficit for Year	Debt Interest for Year	National Debt	Debt Interest as Percent of Budget Deficit
1984		$3,931	4.30%	$185	$111	$1,560	60%
1985	7.29%	$4,218	3.60%	$212	$129	$1,820	61%
1986	5.75%	$4,460	1.90%	$221	$136	$2,120	61%
1987	6.19%	$4,736	3.60%	$150	$139	$2,350	93%
1988	7.69%	$5,100	4.10%	$155	$152	$2,600	98%
1989	7.48%	$5,482	4.80%	$153	$169	$2,870	111%
1990	5.81%	$5,801	5.40%	$221	$184	$3,210	83%
1991	3.30%	$5,992	4.20%	$269	$194	$3,600	72%
1992	5.84%	$6,342	3.00%	$290	$199	$4,000	69%
1993	5.13%	$6,667	3.00%	$255	$199	$4,350	78%
1994	6.27%	$7,085	2.60%	$203	$203	$4,640	100%
1995	4.65%	$7,415	2.80%	$164	$232	$4,920	142%
1996	5.72%	$7,839	3.00%	$107	$241	$5,180	224%
1997	6.30%	$8,332	2.30%	$22	$244	$5,370	1115%
1998	5.53%	$8,794	1.60%	-$69	$241	$5,480	-348%
1999	6.37%	$9,354	2.20%	-$126	$230	$5,610	-183%
2000	6.39%	$9,952	3.40%	-$236	$223	$5,630	-94%
2001	3.36%	$10,286	2.80%	-$128	$206	$5,770	-161%
2002	3.46%	$10,642	1.60%	$158	$171	$6,200	108%
2003	4.70%	$11,142	2.30%	$378	$153	$6,760	41%
2004	6.38%	$11,853	2.70%	$413	$160	$7,350	39%
2005	6.49%	$12,623	3.40%	$318	$184	$7,910	58%
2006	5.97%	$13,377	3.20%	$248	$227	$8,450	91%
2007	4.87%	$14,029	2.80%	$161	$237	$8,950	148%
2008	1.87%	$14,292	3.80%	$459	$253	$9,990	55%
2009	-2.22%	$13,974	-0.40%	$1,413	$187	$11,880	13%
2010	3.76%	$14,499	1.60%	$1,294	$196	$13,530	15%
2011	3.98%	$15,076	3.20%	$1,300	$230	$14,760	18%
2012	4.04%	$15,685	2.10%	$1,087	$220	$16,050	20%
2013	3.30%	$16,203		$680	$221	$16,740	33%

Most of this data was taken from the US Government Spending web site

Note: Figures in billions. Over this period the average GDP growth rate was 5.02 percent, and the average inflation rate was 2.93 percent.

TABLE 4.2. Debt-interest scenarios, 5 percent–8 percent: the next thirty years

	Year	Debt Size	Interest at 5%		Debt Size	Interest at 6%		Debt Size	Interest at 7%		Debt Size	Interest at 8%
0.05	2020	$22,000	$1,100	0.06	$22,000	$1,320	0.07	$22,000	$1,540	0.08	$22,000	$1,760
0.05	2021	$23,100	$1,155	0.06	$23,320	$1,399	0.07	$23,540	$1,648	0.08	$23,760	$1,901
0.05	2022	$24,255	$1,213	0.06	$24,719	$1,483	0.07	$25,188	$1,763	0.08	$25,661	$2,053
0.05	2023	$25,468	$1,273	0.06	$26,202	$1,572	0.07	$26,951	$1,887	0.08	$27,714	$2,217
0.05	2024	$26,741	$1,337	0.06	$27,774	$1,666	0.07	$28,838	$2,019	0.08	$29,931	$2,394
0.05	2025	$28,078	$1,404	0.06	$29,441	$1,766	0.07	$30,856	$2,160	0.08	$32,325	$2,586
0.05	2026	$29,482	$1,474	0.06	$31,207	$1,872	0.07	$33,016	$2,311	0.08	$34,911	$2,793
0.05	2027	$30,956	$1,548	0.06	$33,080	$1,985	0.07	$35,327	$2,473	0.08	$37,704	$3,016
0.05	2028	$32,504	$1,625	0.06	$35,065	$2,104	0.07	$37,800	$2,646	0.08	$40,720	$3,258
0.05	2029	$34,129	$1,706	0.06	$37,169	$2,230	0.07	$40,446	$2,831	0.08	$43,978	$3,518
0.05	2030	$35,836	$1,792	0.06	$39,399	$2,364	0.07	$43,277	$3,029	0.08	$47,496	$3,800
0.05	2031	$37,627	$1,881	0.06	$41,763	$2,506	0.07	$46,307	$3,241	0.08	$51,296	$4,104
0.05	2032	$39,509	$1,975	0.06	$44,268	$2,656	0.07	$49,548	$3,468	0.08	$55,400	$4,432
0.05	2033	$41,484	$2,074	0.06	$46,924	$2,815	0.07	$53,017	$3,711	0.08	$59,832	$4,787
0.05	2034	$43,558	$2,178	0.06	$49,740	$2,984	0.07	$56,728	$3,971	0.08	$64,618	$5,169
0.05	2035	$45,736	$2,287	0.06	$52,724	$3,163	0.07	$60,699	$4,249	0.08	$69,788	$5,583
0.05	2036	$48,023	$2,401	0.06	$55,888	$3,353	0.07	$64,948	$4,546	0.08	$75,371	$6,030
0.05	2037	$50,424	$2,521	0.06	$59,241	$3,554	0.07	$69,494	$4,865	0.08	$81,400	$6,512
0.05	2038	$52,946	$2,647	0.06	$62,795	$3,768	0.07	$74,359	$5,205	0.08	$87,912	$7,033
0.05	2039	$55,593	$2,780	0.06	$66,563	$3,994	0.07	$79,564	$5,569	0.08	$94,945	$7,596
0.05	2040	$58,373	$2,919	0.06	$70,557	$4,233	0.07	$85,133	$5,959	0.08	$102,541	$8,203
0.05	2041	$61,291	$3,065	0.06	$74,790	$4,487	0.07	$91,092	$6,376	0.08	$110,744	$8,860
0.05	2042	$64,356	$3,218	0.06	$79,278	$4,757	0.07	$97,469	$6,823	0.08	$119,604	$9,568
0.05	2043	$67,574	$3,379	0.06	$84,034	$5,042	0.07	$104,292	$7,300	0.08	$129,172	$10,334

What I Believe the Charts Say About...

The figures in these implications have ramifications across the US economy. Following are some of the consequences I foresee.

The National Debt

1. The national debt will have already reached critical mass, and debt interest will gradually become the largest expense in the budget.
2. Interest on the national debt will exceed $1 trillion annually soon after interest rates return to normal (5–6 percent).
3. Within three years, the national debt will exceed $20 trillion.
4. Dumping the annual debt interest and only the debt interest for thirty years into the national debt will cause the debt to grow to between $65 trillion and $125 trillion by 2043.

5. Dumping budget shortfalls from both discretionary and nondiscretionary programs, in addition to debt interest, for thirty years will push the debt to even-higher levels—tens of trillions of dollars at a minimum.

The Government

1. The government has no stomach for taking the necessary steps to balance the budget and will continue to spend well in excess of the revenue it receives.
2. We will not be able to grow our way out of the national debt crisis, because GDP growth will be nowhere near enough to offset the growth caused by budget deficits.
3. If interest rates had been at normal rates for the last six years, debt interest would now be at least $1 trillion annually and account for more than 25 percent of the entire current budget.
4. Bond vigilantes will see weakness, sell short, and dump their securities onto the open market, causing rates to spike out of control. This will force the US government to restructure its debt, resulting in a partial default.
5. The major rating agencies will downgrade US debt as the debt load becomes more-and-more unmanageable, which will force higher interest rates and budget deficits.

The Federal Reserve

1. The Federal Reserve's low-rate policy has enabled the government to mask the seriousness of the national-debt crisis.
2. The Fed's attempt to force low interest rates by purchasing large quantities of bonds will eventually prove useless as they lose their credibility.
3. The Fed's ability to fight inflation will be severely hampered because upward interest-rate adjustments on the huge national debt will create massive budget deficits and massive increases in debt interest.

4. Accommodative interest rates enabled the government to continue to incur massive budget deficits while paying minimal debt interest.

Owning Up to the Crisis

1. The government will not act on the national-debt crisis until it is forced to buy out-of-control interest rates.
2. Massive budget cuts will severely affect all spending programs, including defense, government pensions, and entitlements.
3. The United States and most of the free world will undergo a severe recession.
4. Unemployment will skyrocket.
5. The stock market will lose at least half its value, and interest rates will soar.
6. Social unrest will result from massive cuts in all government programs.

The Government's Attitude Problem

The budget sequestration act put into effect in 2013 forced the government to reduce spending by $85 billion. President Obama and his supporters cried foul and inferred that the Republican wing of Congress was heartlessly cutting important spending programs, and citizens would suffer the consequences. It was all nonsense, of course, but it does highlight the Democratic Party's resistance to fiscal discipline. How do you think the party would react to $1.5 trillion in austerity measures, an amount seventeen times greater than the $85 billion about which it previously panicked?

The Uninformed American

Throughout this book, I have identified many reasons why the national debt is such a serious problem. In my opinion, one of the biggest problems is that the general public doesn't even know it is a problem. Our political leaders spend money like drunken sailors—in the last seven years, they paid out $1 trillion a year more than the country receives in tax revenues. The national debt is one of the most misunderstood problems facing America. It doesn't get anywhere near the amount of the attention it deserves. The media avoids it because it's a very complex issue and as they often say, we "don't want to get into the weeds." Politicians also prefer keeping the issue out of the limelight for obvious reasons. If Congress didn't need to periodically increase the debt ceiling, the issue would almost never be in the news.

It is commonly believed that the biggest problem with the national debt is its size. Of course size is a big problem, but in fact it is only part of the problem. Even more important are interest rates, or to put it another way, the amount it will cost taxpayers to fund the debt.

Up to this point, I have been explaining the parts all of the major players had in creating the $18 trillion national debt. I explained how politicians regard the national debt as free money and use it to fund their political ideologies as well local pork-funded projects, creating budget deficits in record numbers. I showed how the credit agencies overrate government debt. Later in this book, I show how the government intimidated S&P after its downgrade of US debt in 2008. In my opinion, the intimidation of S&P by the government is the main reason Moody's and the Fitch Group still maintain their top rating on US debt. I showed that if an individual sported the same income, expense, and debt ratios as the government, no bank would lend it ten cents. I showed that fixing the national debt problem is next to impossible and that reducing it through economic growth, spending cuts, or tax increases is just a pipe dream. And I showed the power of the Federal Reserve Bank and its ability to almost completely control interest rates and determine the cost of financing the debt.

I personally consider this next paragraph the most important paragraph in the book, because in it, to the best of my ability, I explain why the national debt problem is of no concern to the general public. Here is my explanation of growing the debt without pain:

By 2014, the national debt had grown by about 80 percent, to almost $18 trillion, from about $10 trillion in 2008. The Fed's low interest rate policy was in effect *throughout the period, yet the amount of debt interest paid barely budged from year to year. This was made possible by the fact that debt issued prior to the Fed's low-rate policy yielded higher rates and upon maturity was rolled over (reissued) at the current low rates. This had the effect of keeping the growth of the national debt out of the public eye, as the government was able to increase the size of the national debt massively without having to increase a comparable amount of debt interest.*

Figure 4.1 illustrates the interest rate paid on national debt from 1988 through 2014. Note the effect of the Federal Reserve's low interest rate policy on debt interest payments from the start of the 2007–2008 recession until the present. It was almost cut in half from 4.80 percent to 2.42 percent. The table that follows, table 4.3, backs up the graph with actual numbers. Don't be fooled into thinking that rates dropped steadily from 1988 to the present. If I showed the stats for the last fifty years, you would see rates bouncing around, reflecting the economic conditions of the period. On average, interest rates over that fifty-year period were close to 6 percent.

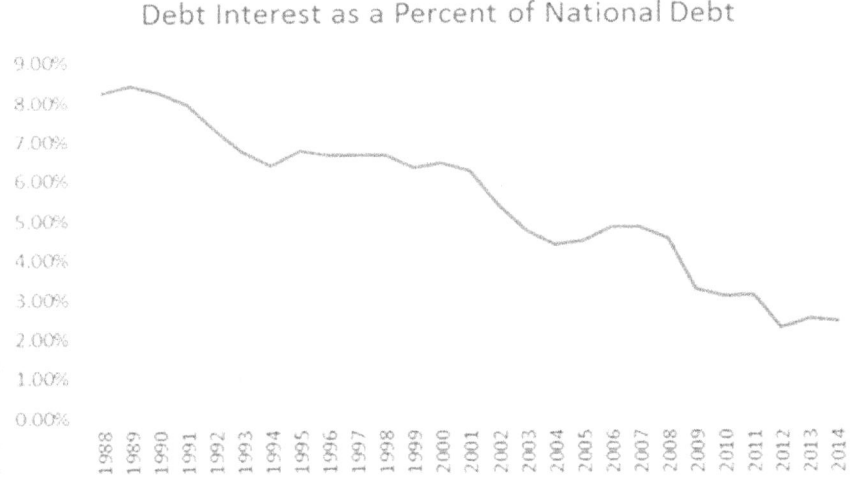

Figure 4.1. The growth of the national debt and the decrease in interest rates.

TABLE 4.3. National debt statistics, 1988–2014

Year	Revenues	Budget Expenses	Budget Defisit	Debt Interest	National Debt	Debt Int. as % of Nat. Debt
2014	$3,021	$3,506	($485)	$431	$17,794	2.42%
2013	$2,775	$3,455	($680)	$416	$16,719	2.49%
2012	$2,450	$3,537	($1,087)	$360	$16,050	2.24%
2011	$2,303	$3,603	($1,300)	$454	$14,764	3.08%
2010	$2,163	$3,457	($1,294)	$414	$13,529	3.06%
2009	$2,105	$3,518	($1,413)	$383	$11,876	3.23%
2008	$2,524	$2,983	($459)	$451	$9,986	4.52%
2007	$2,568	$2,729	($161)	$430	$8,951	4.80%
2006	$2,407	$2,655	($248)	$406	$8,451	4.80%
2005	$2,154	$2,472	($318)	$352	$7,905	4.46%
2004	$1,880	$2,293	($413)	$322	$7,355	4.37%
2003	$1,782	$2,160	($378)	$318	$6,760	4.71%
2002	$1,853	$2,011	($158)	$333	$6,198	5.37%
2001	$1,991	$1,863	$128	$360	$5,770	6.23%
2000	$2,025	$1,789	$236	$362	$5,629	6.43%
1999	$1,827	$1,702	$126	$354	$5,605	6.31%
1998	$1,722	$1,652	$69	$364	$5,478	6.64%
1997	$1,579	$1,601	($22)	$356	$5,369	6.63%
1996	$1,453	$1,560	($107)	$344	$5,181	6.64%
1995	$1,352	$1,516	($164)	$332	$4,921	6.76%
1994	$1,259	$1,462	($203)	$296	$4,643	6.38%
1993	$1,154	$1,409	($255)	$293	$4,351	6.72%
1992	$1,091	$1,382	($290)	$292	$4,002	7.31%
1991	$1,055	$1,324	($269)	$286	$3,598	7.95%
1990	$1,032	$1,253	($221)	$265	$3,216	8.24%
1989	$991	$1,144	($153)	$241	$2,868	8.40%
1988	$909	$1,064	($155)	$214	$2,601	8.23%

In Billions

The Federal Reserve's low interest rate policy put into effect in 2008 had a dramatic effect on the cost of funding the national debt. In 2008, it cost taxpayers $459 billion to fund a $10 trillion national debt. In the following six years, the debt grew by more than $1 trillion a year, skyrocketing from $10 trillion to $17.8 trillion by 2014, yet in only one of those years did debt interest exceed that same $459 billion. The Federal Reserve kept the average interest rate at about 1.3 percent throughout the period, so in spite of the fact that the debt was growing by leaps and bounds, the full cost of funding the debt averaged just $415 billion a year, changing very little from year to year. Is it any wonder that the general public as well as the media remained oblivious to the growth of the debt? Had interest rates remained near the norm of the last fifty years or so, at around 6 percent, the cost of funding the debt would have been in excess of $1 trillion annually. That means it would have cost taxpayers one-fourth to one-third of all tax revenues just to fund the debt. Any civic-minded person would have been up in arms about the huge cost of funding the debt. In my opinion, the government's secret is safe until the Federal Reserve normalizes interest rates.

Did the Federal Reserve Go Too Far?

On August 24th, 2015, the Dow Jones Industrial Average had its first-ever one-thousand-point intraday loss. That loss occurred during a four- or five-week period of increased market volatility, where, at its low point, the Dow lost more than two thousand points. The volatility was the result of a foreign exchange move by China, which devalued its currency, the yuan, by about 3 percent. Stock markets worldwide suffered major losses on concerns that China's economy was in a funk and the devaluation indicated a prolonged period of weak growth. There was fear that the economies of China's trading partners would also be negatively affected.

Market gurus were in panic mode because they were concerned that the Federal Reserve had boxed itself into a corner with the zero-interest-rate policy it put into effect to combat the 2008 recession. They were concerned that the Fed's ability to spur economic growth through monetary policy changes was no longer a given. Even with a near-zero-interest-rate policy and budget deficits averaging over $1 trillion a year, the economy had grown at an anemic rate of about 2 percent annually since the 2008 recession.

The Federal Reserve purchased about $4 trillion in Treasury and mortgage-backed securities to insure that rates remained near zero. Be careful what you wish for! This China devaluation scare raises the question, With rates already at zero and the Fed owning $4 trillion in securities, what would be left in the Fed's arsenal if it needed to act to fight another recession?

The Creditworthiness of the United States

The vast majority of Americans consider Treasury securities one of the safest investments on the planet. After all, they're backed by the "full faith and credit of the US government." Unfortunately that guarantee isn't worth what it used to be. Up until August 2011, all government-issued securities carried the highest-possible rating by the three major rating agencies. It is now down to two credit agencies.

The Bogus Employment Picture and the Big 4 Percent

While I believe the Department of Labor's statistics grossly misrepresent the true labor picture, the one statistic I do believe is the labor participation rate. The details of this statistic are unknown to me, but that's not important. What matters is the trend, which has been heading south since 2002, when it was 67 percent, and has accelerated downward under the Obama administration to 63 percent, a thirty-year low.

As shown in figure 4.2, this 4 percent difference has a major effect on the state of the economy. With a 63 percent participation rate, it takes about 63 percent to support the other 37 percent. With the civilian labor force at about 155 million, that 4 percent difference equates to more than five million jobs lost. Now we have five million fewer workers to support the American economy, plus the added cost of supporting five million nonworking Americans. I confess to a lack of expertise in the field of economics, but I am fairly certain this stat is mostly overlooked and has a much larger detrimental effect on the economy than is generally known.

Figure 4.2. The eight-hundred-pound gorilla in the room.

Another hole in the employment picture is the way the unemployment rate is calculated. Individuals who lose their job are counted as unemployed. As soon as they stop looking for a new job, they are no longer considered unemployed by the Bureau of Labor Statistics. The deciding factor is the state of mind of the former employee and how he or she views his job prospects. How stupid is that? If you're capable of working and are not working, you're unemployed. Period! Who would believe that encouraging an unemployed person to look for work would cause the unemployment rate to rise? In other words, it benefits the party in power to discourage unemployed workers from seeking employment because their admission of interest in finding a job raises the employment rate. More stupidity!

All that being said, these problems are minor when compared to the national debt, the interest needed to fund it, and the massive and perpetual budget deficits it will create. There is no doubt the national debt is the eight-hundred-pound gorilla in the room, but what is totally mind blowing is that the gorilla goes mostly unnoticed. As I said previously, politicians downplay the issue, the media ignores it, and most taxpayers have not knowingly paid ten cents toward the reduction of the national debt.

The Debt Interest Explosion

Of course, predicting budgets thirty years into the future is foolish. The uncertainties are boundless. However, the issues surrounding the national debt are quantifiable, and we can make predictions using various scenarios. There are four factors to consider: the cost of ongoing government programs, the cost of interest needed to fund the national debt, the size of the national debt, and interest rates. *As the national debt grows, it will become the defining factor in the growth of the budget and budget deficits.* Growth from ongoing and new government programs will become less and less of a factor.

When Will Interest Rates Return to Normal?

The Federal Reserve has all the power to decide when interest rates will return to normal, as it is an independent agency not answerable to the president or Congress. The party in power exerts enormous pressure on the Fed to keep rates low in order to stimulate the economy, spur employment, and minimize budget deficits. On the other side of the coin, the Fed is under pressure to push rates higher when inflation rears its ugly head. As the economy has been in the tank since the 2007 housing bust, the Fed has kept rates at record lows and promises to continue this policy until it is satisfied with the state of the economy and the unemployment rate.

Fed action on interest rates has enormous consequences. On a $20 trillion debt, every one-point rise in interest rates equates to $200 billion in additional debt interest. Moving rates from the current average of 2 percent to a normal average of 6 percent will increase debt interest by $800 billion annually over the long term.

If the thirty-year Treasury bond is at risk of default prior to maturity, as I believe it is, rising interest rates will be the primary reason. The CBO expects the national debt to hit the $20 trillion mark by 2016 or 2017. Bear in mind there is more to budget deficits than just debt interest. In 2013, debt interest was responsible for only one-third of the budget deficit. Since I am certain the Obama administration, currently in power, will do next to nothing to address the never-ending budget deficits and growing national debt, I expect almost all the budget overruns to be dumped onto the national debt. If, as I expect, this scenario plays out continuously for twenty-three more years, through 2043, the national debt will reach $60 to $120 trillion, and that's without including deficits from other budget programs. Also bear in mind that over the last thirty years, the budget grew at twice the rate of inflation.

As the national debt reaches $40, $50, and $60 trillion, or more, and our country's credit rating falls, investors will demand ever-higher interest rates to compensate for the added risk. The outlook for this country's credit rating is dim. The political and economic winds are blowing in the wrong direction.

The Path to Armageddon

Debt interest in 2013 should have been more than four times greater than what we actually paid, or roughly $1.1 trillion instead of the current estimate of $250 billion. The average interest rate for the forty-year period prior to the Fed's "easy-money" policy was about 6 percent. If interest rates were allowed to float, the average rate would probably be even higher due to the growth of the national debt and the declining creditworthiness of the United States.

Let's start in the year 2020 with an estimated national debt of $22 trillion and an estimated budget deficit of $700 billion. (How I derived this debt amount for 2020 is explained in the previous section "Countdown to Armageddon.") Add to that amount $850 billion to cover the increased debt interest resulting from the return to normal interest rates. That's $850 billion more than the $250 billion we paid in 2013, while the Fed's low-rate policy was in effect. These two items taken together bring the 2020 budget deficit to more than $1.5 trillion. So unless the government cuts spending or raises taxes to meet this budget shortfall, we will add this $1.5 trillion to the national debt, which would bring it to $23.5 trillion. (Note: A 5 percent interest rate on a $22 trillion debt equates to $1.1 trillion in interest.)

Because the national debt is financed by Treasury securities of various maturities, ranging from the one-year Treasury bill to the thirty-year Treasury bond, interest rate changes will not affect the entire debt all at once. Rate changes will affect 40 percent of the debt in the first year, 55 percent in the second year, 70 percent in the third year, 76 percent in the fourth year, 82 percent in the fifth year, and so on. The example I just cited will start in 2020, so I assume this interest-rate lag will not have a material effect.

Stay with me on this! In the following year, 2021, we have the same problem except that we have to pay debt interest on a national debt of $23.5 trillion instead of $22 trillion. This will require adding another $1.5 trillion to the national debt to cover the previous year's deficit and an additional $82 billion to cover the extra debt interest caused by the previous year's increase in the debt. This raises the national debt to over $25 trillion. Try to visualize the disaster facing our country if our government takes no action is on the debt crisis, and this scenario plays out continuously for another twenty-one years, through 2043. Ugh!

In May of 2013, the Congressional Budget Office (CBO) issued the following forecast: "CBO estimates a 2015 deficit of $378 billion. However, the cumulative effect in the next decade of deficit spending through 2023 is projected to be $6.3 trillion." Even the CBO, which has a long history of underestimating government expenditures, is predicting an average budget deficit of $630 billion annually from 2014 through 2023.

Figure 4.3, produced by the CBO, shows its version of the long-term cost of funding the national debt as a percent of GDP.

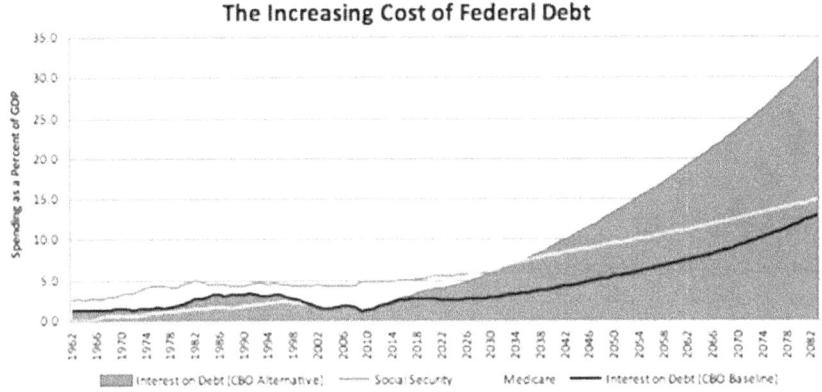

Figure 4.3.

Figure 4.4 shows the CBO's estimate of the size of the national debt in relation to the nation's GDP through 2035 under various scenarios. I am not aware of the data that backs up these scenarios, but that's not important. In the worst-case scenario, the national debt-to-GDP ratio exceeds 180 percent. That's a higher ratio than Greece had when the country had to default on 50 percent of its sovereign debt because it could not meet the debt burden.

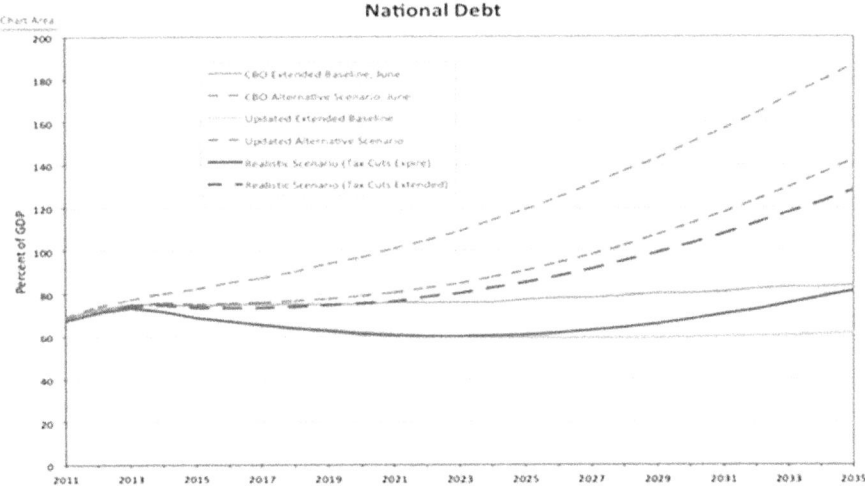

Figure 4.4.

I believe the figure I started with in 2020, indicating an estimated *budget deficit* of $700 billion, is realistic. The $850 billion in *additional debt interest* from the return to normal rates is not an estimate; it is factual. The interest is simply a mathematical calculation. In fact, I think I may be understating future interest rates, because the 5 percent rate is more than likely too low and assumes a top credit rating. In my opinion, in order for investors to accept a 5 percent interest rate, the United States would need a stable budget and a manageable national debt in addition to a top credit rating. None of these exist now, nor is there any reason to believe they will any time soon.

Doing the Math

In table 4.2, "Debt-interest Scenarios, 5 Percent–8 Percent: The Next Thirty Years," we looked at the projected growth of the national debt from 2020 through 2043 at various interest rates. I started with a national debt of $22 trillion and compounded it each year for the twenty-three-year period. I showed the effect of the growing debt using four different interest rates, from 5 percent through 8 percent. The figure worked out to $67 trillion in 2043 at a 5 percent annual interest rate and jumped to $84 trillion at a 6 percent rate, $104 trillion at a 7 percent rate, and $129 trillion at an 8 percent rate. Bear in mind that these figures are based solely on the growth of the national debt resulting from debt interest and do not factor in additional spending from any new or expanded government programs in the future. Add in the latter, and it could boost the 2043 national debt by another 25 percent, to 50 percent. Under these scenarios, the annual debt interest amounts in 2043 range from $3 trillion to more than $10 trillion. Ouch! Remember, we are talking about a future national debt anywhere between $67 trillion and $129 trillion.

The Effects of Inflation

You could argue that the situation in 2043 may wind up the same as a result of inflation, or that we could just grow our way out of the national debt problem. These are not the answers. Government spending exceeds the growth in inflation by a wide margin. Over the last thirty years, inflation rose by a total of 88 percent, or by about 2.9 percent annually. During that same period the US budget grew by 470 percent, or about 5.3 percent annually. In 1983, the US budget was $808 billion, as compared to $3.8 trillion in 2012.

Table 4.4, showing the inflation rate by year, goes all the way back to 1967. Note that the interest rates in the 1970s and early 1980s were much higher due to runaway inflation associated with a sharp increase in the price of oil. If you include all the years going back to 1967, the inflation rate for the entire forty-five-year period would be just over 5 percent. At a 3 percent annual inflation rate, a $22 trillion national debt in 2020 would grow to $43 trillion by 2043. At a 5 percent rate, it would grow to $67 trillion.

TABLE 4.4. Inflation rates, 1967–2012

Year	Inflation Rate	Year	Inflation Rate	Year	Inflation Rate	Year	Inflation Rate
1967	3.10%	1979	11.30%	1990	5.40%	2002	1.60%
1968	4.20%	1980	13.50%	1991	4.20%	2003	2.30%
1969	5.50%	1981	10.30%	1992	3.00%	2004	2.70%
1970	5.70%	1982	6.20%	1993	3.00%	2005	3.40%
1971	4.40%	1983	3.20%	1994	2.60%	2006	3.20%
1972	3.20%	1984	4.30%	1995	2.80%	2007	2.80%
1973	6.20%	1985	3.60%	1996	3.00%	2008	3.80%
1974	11.00%	1986	1.90%	1997	2.30%	2009	-0.40%
1975	9.10%	1987	3.60%	1998	1.60%	2010	1.60%
1976	5.80%	1988	4.10%	1999	2.20%	2011	3.20%
1977	6.50%	1989	4.80%	2000	3.40%	2012	2.10%
1978	7.60%			2001	2.80%		

Table 4.5 shows the growth of the budget over the thirty years prior to 2013. This is followed by table 4.6, showing what the budget will be in the next thirty years if budget growth continues at the same rate. In addition, there is a side-by-side comparison of the actual growth rate of 5.3 percent and what the budget would be if it grew at the 2.9 percent rate of inflation. The table forecasts a budget of $17.9 trillion at the 5.3 percent growth rate

thirty years down the road, in 2043, and about $9 trillion if the budget grew only at the 2.9 percent rate of inflation.

TABLE 4.5. Revenues, expenses, budget deficits, and GDP, 1983–2013

Year	GDP	Budget Deficit	Total Revenues	Total Expenses		Year	GDP	Budget Deficit	Total Revenues	Total Expenses
	In Billions	In Billions	In Billions	In Billions			In Billions	In Billions	In Billions	In Billions
2013	$16,300	$901	$2,900	$3,800 *****		1997	$8,210	$22	$1,580	$1,600
2012	$15,600	$1,380	$2,470	$3,800 *****		1996	$7,720	$107	$1,450	$1,560
2011	$15,000	$1,300	$2,300	$3,600 *****		1995	$7,340	$164	$1,350	$1,520
2010	$14,500	$1,290	$2,160	$3,460 *****		1994	$6,980	$203	$1,260	$1,460
2009	$14,200	$1,410	$2,100	$3,520 *****		1993	$6,590	$255	$1,150	$1,410
2008	$14,400	$459	$2,520	$2,980 *****		1992	$6,240	$290	$1,090	$1,380
2007	$13,900	$161	$2,570	$2,730 *****		1991	$5,930	$269	$1,060	$1,320
2006	$13,200	$248	$2,410	$2,660 *****		1990	$5,730	$221	$1,030	$1,250
2005	$12,400	$318	$2,150	$2,470 *****		1989	$5,400	$153	$991	$1,140
2004	$11,700	$413	$1,880	$2,290 *****		1988	$5,010	$155	$909	$1,060
2003	$11,000	$378	$1,780	$2,160 *****		1987	$4,650	$150	$854	$1,000
2002	$10,500	$158	$1,850	$2,010 *****		1986	$4,400	$221	$769	$990
2001	$10,200	($128)	$1,990	$1,860 *****		1985	$4,150	$212	$734	$946
2000	$9,820	($236)	$2,030	$1,790 *****		1984	$3,840	$185	$666	$852
1999	$9,210	($126)	$1,830	$1,700 *****		1983	$3,440	$208	$601	$808
1998	$8,660	($69)	$1,720	$1,650 *****						

TABLE 4.6. A comparison of estimated budgets for 2014 to 2043 using both the growth rates of the actual budgets (5.3 percent) and the rate of inflation (2.9 percent) over the last thirty years

Year	Budget Growth at Last 30-Yr. Average Rate 5.3%	Budget Growth at 30-Yr. Inflation Rate of 2.9%	Year	Budget Growth at Last 30-Yr. Average Rate 5.3%	Budget Growth at 30-Yr. Inflation Rate of 2.9%	Year	Budget Growth at Last 30-Yr. Average Rate 5.3%	Budget Growth at 30-Yr. Inflation Rate of 2.9%
2014	$4,006	$3,915	2024	$6,714	$5,210	2034	$11,253	$6,934
2015	$4,218	$4,028	2025	$7,070	$5,361	2035	$11,849	$7,135
2016	$4,442	$4,145	2026	$7,444	$5,516	2036	$12,477	$7,342
2017	$4,677	$4,265	2027	$7,839	$5,676	2037	$13,138	$7,555
2018	$4,925	$4,389	2028	$8,254	$5,841	2038	$13,835	$7,774
2019	$5,186	$4,516	2029	$8,692	$6,010	2039	$14,568	$7,999
2020	$5,461	$4,647	2030	$9,153	$6,185	2040	$15,340	$8,231
2021	$5,750	$4,782	2031	$9,638	$6,364	2041	$16,153	$8,470
2022	$6,055	$4,920	2032	$10,148	$6,549	2042	$17,009	$8,716
2023	$6,376	$5,063	2033	$10,686	$6,739	2043	$17,911	$8,969

Table 4.7 shows how fast the debt will rise based on three different inflation rate levels. Here I start with the 2013 national debt of $16.7 trillion and calculate how large the debt would be if it grew at a 3 percent, 4 percent, and 5 percent inflation rate. Bear in mind that we are talking about the rate of inflation, and not about interest rates. The table shows that at a steady 3 percent inflation rate, by 2043 the debt would grow to over $40 trillion; at a 4 percent inflation rate, the debt would grow to $54 trillion; and at 5 percent inflation rate, it would grow to S72 trillion. On the surface, these numbers may look insane, and they are insane. As insane as they appear, though, they are real and the result of an insane situation brought on by out-of-control government spending.

TABLE 4.7.

National Debt
30 Year Growth Rate

	3.00% Inflation Rate	4.00% Inflation Rate	5.00% Inflation Rate
2013	$16,740	$16,740	$16,740
2014	$17,242	$17,410	$17,577
2015	$17,759	$18,106	$18,456
2016	$18,292	$18,830	$19,379
2017	$18,841	$19,583	$20,348
2018	$19,406	$20,367	$21,365
2019	$19,988	$21,181	$22,433
2020	$20,588	$22,029	$23,555
2021	$21,206	$22,910	$24,733
2022	$21,842	$23,826	$25,969
2023	$22,497	$24,779	$27,268
2024	$23,172	$25,770	$28,631
2025	$23,867	$26,801	$30,063
2026	$24,583	$27,873	$31,566
2027	$25,321	$28,988	$33,144
2028	$26,080	$30,148	$34,801
2029	$26,863	$31,354	$36,541
2030	$27,669	$32,608	$38,368
2031	$28,499	$33,912	$40,287
2032	$29,354	$35,269	$42,301
2033	$30,234	$36,679	$44,416
2034	$31,141	$38,147	$46,637
2035	$32,076	$39,672	$48,969
2036	$33,038	$41,259	$51,417
2037	$34,029	$42,910	$53,988
2038	$35,050	$44,626	$56,688
2039	$36,101	$46,411	$59,522
2040	$37,184	$48,268	$62,498
2041	$38,300	$50,198	$65,623
2042	$39,449	$52,206	$68,904
2043	$40,632	$54,294	$72,349

Business as Usual

If it was possible to shock the reader about the severity of the national debt crisis, this next table would be the one to do it. I call table 4.8 "Business as Usual?" because it brings home in spades the potential results of one of the most important questions I've been trying to ask: What will happen if our country does nothing about the national debt and continues its current policy of heavy reliance on the debt as the path of least resistance for obtaining the funds needed to meet budget shortfalls? The out-of-sight, out-of-mind attitude put forth by our political leadership successfully convinced taxpayers that the national debt is not a serious problem. As a result, the political leadership has felt no pressure to take action. In the thirty years from 1984 through 2013, the national debt grew by 1073 percent, from $1.5 trillion to $16.7 trillion. If the growth rate of the last thirty years were applied to the next thirty years 2013 to 2043, the national debt would grow from $16.7 trillion to an astronomical, mind-blowing $180 trillion. That's right—$180 trillion.

TABLE 4.8. Business as usual?

1984 National Debt	$1.560 Trillion
2013 National Debt	$16.740 Trillion
2043 National Debt	$179.630 Trillion

You may be tempted to point out that the debt ballooned over the last six years because of the trillion-dollar budget deficits resulting from the very weak economy that began with the 2008 recession, suggesting that this current economic recovery is one of the slowest on record. Let me add this: In a normal economy, it is likely the majority of those deficits would still have been there, as the deficits were due mostly to expensive government programs that were unrelated to the recession. These expenses would have only been partially offset by additional income from an improved economy. The only borrowing the government actually did that was tied to the recession was the $700 billion Troubled Asset Relief Program (TARP) in 2008 and the $787 billion American Recovery and Reinvestment Act (ARRA) in 2009. In addition, because of the recession the Federal Reserve kept interest rates at record lows. In my opinion, these rate reductions saved the government about $2.7 trillion since the 2008 recession or about $550 billion a year. The savings came solely from the reduced cost of funding the national debt. So as I see it, as outrageous as these numbers look, they are realistic.

The Race to Armageddon

I want to now show you the national debt problem from a different perspective—the perspective of time. As the general population doesn't appear to be concerned about the size of the national debt, we must assume that they certainly do not have a clue about how fast it has grown. Figure 4.5 is a comparison between various economic growth rates and the actual growth rate of the national debt from 1983 to 2013. Note that the growth rate of the national debt far outpaced the growth rate of any of these economic benchmarks by a wide margin. The annual growth rate of the national debt over the last thirty years was 8.4 percent, almost three times the rate of inflation (2.9 percent), and more than one-and-a-half times both the average GDP growth rate (5.2 percent) and the average growth rate of government spending (5.3 percent). This is the same period that saw the national debt grow from $1.57 trillion to $17.65 trillion.

Economic Growth Rates

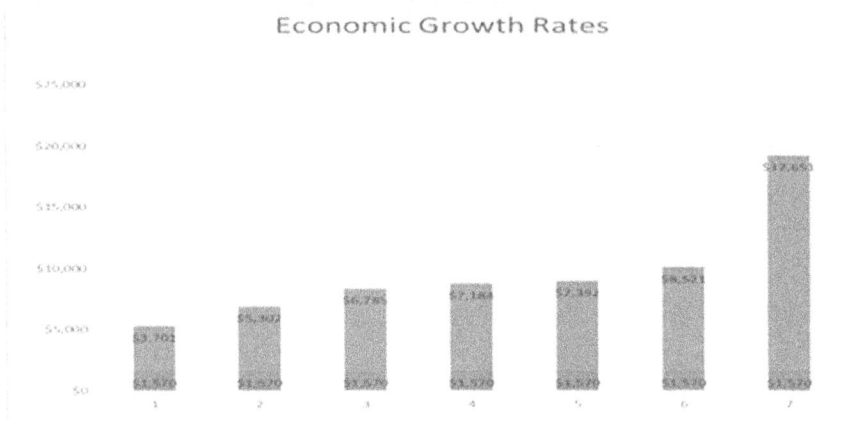

Figure 4.5.

Note: Economic growth rates (*x*-axis):

1 = 2.9 percent Average inflation rate from 1983 to 2013

2 = 4.1 percent average interest rate needed to fund the national debt from 1988 to 2015 (inclusive of the Fed's zero-interest-rate policy from 2008 to the August 2015)

3 = 5.0 percent average inflation rate from 1967 to 2013

4 = 5.2 percent average GDP growth rate from 1984 to 2013

5 = 5.3 percent average rate of annual budget increases from 1983 to 2013

6 = 5.8 percent average interest rate needed to fund the national debt from 1988 to 2007

7 = 8.4 percent compounded growth rate of the national debt for this 30 year period from 1983 to 2013

Table 4.9 shows the actual annual growth rate in dollars of the national debt from 1984 to 2013. Note the heavy reliance on deficit spending since the start of the 2007 recession, averaging over $1 trillion a year. From 2007 through 2015, in just eight years, the national debt doubled from $9 trillion to $18 trillion.

TABLE 4.9.

Actual Annual Growth in National Debt
1984 - 2013

Year	National Debt	Annual Increase	Percent Increase		Year	National Debt	Annual Increase	Percent Increase
30-Sep-84	$1,570	$250	* * * *		30-Sep-99	$5,650	$20	2.36%
30-Sep-85	$1,820	$300	15.92% * * * *		30-Sep-00	$5,670	$130	0.35%
30-Sep-86	$2,120	$230	16.48% * * * *		30-Sep-01	$5,800	$420	2.29%
30-Sep-87	$2,350	$250	10.85% * * * *		30-Sep-02	$6,220	$560	7.24%
30-Sep-88	$2,600	$250	10.64% * * * *		30-Sep-03	$6,780	$590	9.00%
29-Sep-89	$2,850	$380	9.62% * * * *		30-Sep-04	$7,370	$550	8.70%
28-Sep-90	$3,230	$430	13.33% * * * *		30-Sep-05	$7,920	$580	7.46%
30-Sep-91	$3,660	$400	13.31% * * * *		30-Sep-06	$8,500	$500	7.32%
30-Sep-92	$4,060	$350	10.93% * * * *		30-Sep-07	$9,000	$1,020	5.88%
30-Sep-93	$4,410	$280	8.62% * * * *		30-Sep-08	$10,020	$1,880	11.33%
30-Sep-94	$4,690	$280	6.35% * * * *		30-Sep-09	$11,900	$1,660	18.76%
29-Sep-95	$4,970	$250	5.97% * * * *		30-Sep-10	$13,560	$1,230	13.95%
30-Sep-96	$5,220	$190	5.03% * * * *		30-Sep-11	$14,790	$1,270	9.07%
30-Sep-97	$5,410	$110	3.64% * * * *		30-Sep-12	$16,060	$670	8.59%
30-Sep-98	$5,520	$130	2.03% * * * *		30-Sep-13	$16,730	$1,094	4.17%
					30-Sep-14	$17,824		6.54%

In Billions   treasurydirect.gov

Stalking a Wounded Animal

The growing debt and deficit problem will have consequences well beyond the tax bill. America's inability to manage its finances has already resulted in a credit downgrade by S&P. The growing national debt problem makes further downgrades all but inevitable. Credit downgrades force bond issuers to pay higher interest rates to compensate for the higher risk.

In order to guarantee low rates in spite of the credit downgrades, the Federal Reserve plays games (shilling for the government) by purchasing more than $1 trillion a year in Treasury and mortgage-backed securities, trumping the higher rates disgruntled investors demand. Normally, in a rising interest rate environment, investors would sell bonds short with the goal of repurchasing them at lower prices brought on by the higher rates.

In my opinion, this is a flawed strategy, because as the national debt grows, the Fed's strategy will lose credibility. Investors worldwide will see a weaker America and back off from buying US government securities unless interest rates are raised to reflect their true risk. Which investors would be willing to lend the United States money at the current low rate of under 4 percent for thirty years, when we carry a national debt near the size of the GDP of the entire European Union?

Where money is involved, there are no nice guys. The weaker America's credit becomes, the faster bond vigilantes will pounce. Investors of every kind will run from US bonds, ranging from pension funds to sovereign nations. This will force the Treasury to keep boosting rates and start a cycle of increasing budget deficits and an expanding national debt.

(Note: The term *bond vigilante* is used to describe bond traders who look for opportunities to make money by selling bonds short. These traders range from brokers, banks, and fund managers, to sovereign nations. They are known for rushing in to sell large sums of bonds of a country that is in financial trouble. They expect that nation to keep increasing their interest rates as their economies deteriorate in order to keep selling their newly issued sovereign debt. This gives the bond vigilantes the opportunity to cash in by buying back the bonds they had previously sold at a higher price. The nation that is in financial trouble usually condemns this action because bond vigilantes put added pressure on the nation's debt, making it more difficult for that nation to stabilize its economy.)

The Federal Reserve is, in fact, the sovereign bank of the United States. The sovereign bank of Greece was unable to prevent the default of Greek government bonds, and bondholders lost 50 percent of their principal investments. Spain and Italy also got into similar trouble and were able to prevent a crisis only because of the European Union's intervention. There is no entity on earth with the financial resources needed to bail out the US Treasury. Should the debt crisis get out of control, the United States will face a financial Armageddon. Table 4.10 shows the S&P ratings of the different countries and the outlook given.

TABLE 4.10. Sample of some S&P ratings and outlooks and GDP-debt ratios

Country	Rating	Outlook	2006	2007	2008	2009	2010	2011	2012	2013	2014	2015	2016
US	AA-	Negative	61.1	62.2	71.2	84.6	91.6	99.5	102.9	105.6	107.5	109.4	111.9
China	AA-	Stable	16.2	19.6	17	17.7	17.7	17.1	16.3	15	13.4	10.8	9.7
Greece	CC	Negative	106.1	105.1	110.3	126.8	142	152.3	157.7	157	152.5	149.4	145.5
Italy	A-	Negative	106.6	103.6	106.3	116.1	119	120.3	120	119.7	119.3	118.7	118
Spain	AA	Negative	39.6	36.1	39.8	53.2	60.1	63.9	67.1	69.9	72.1	74.1	75.9
Germany	AAA	Stable	67.6	64.9	66.3	73.5	80	80.1	79.4	77.9	75.8	73.8	71.9

Uncle Sam: The Honeymoon is Over!

"Hi, my name is Ralph. My wife Alice and I have been happily married for twenty-five years. My wife and I love each other very much but we argue almost every day. For reasons unknown to me, my wife thinks I'm irresponsible. I drive a city bus for a living and make a salary of $30,000 a year. I'm pretty much on the low end of the economic scale, but I think big. I'm an idea guy. I am constantly coming up with new ideas to make money. I got some of my best ideas from Ralph Kramden on his old TV series *The Honeymooners*. It starred Jackie Gleason, Art Carney, Audrey Meadows, and Joyce Randolph.

"I borrowed $70,000 to buy a warehouse full of what I call "the helpful housewife happy handy kitchen gadget." I wisely took out a live TV ad and played the "chef of the future" to advertise it. Sadly, my idea flopped and I lost my entire investment. Never one to give up, I got an inside tip about a movie theater going up. So I borrowed $100,000 and bought a parking lot next door. Unfortunately it turned out to be a drive-in theater. Rats! Now I owe $170,000 that has to be repaid soon. If I can ever get out of debt, I'm thinking about investing in wallpaper that glows in the dark so people can save money on electricity. Will you consider lending me the $170,000 so I can pay off my loan? I admit that I am having a little trouble paying my bills. In fact, this year I will need to borrow another $6,400 to make ends meet. If you think I'm a good credit risk, please lend the money to me. I promise I will pay back every penny, although I have no idea how. Here's a list of my income and expenses.

Income and Expenses for Ralph and Alice

Expenses		Income	
College Tuition	$9,100	Salary	$30,000
Medical Insurance	$9,700	New Loan	$6,400
Private education	$1,100		
Real estate tax	$4,000		
Mortgage payment	$8,200		
Home security	$500		
Transportation	$1,000		
Loan Interest	$2,200		
Other	$600		Other
Totals	$36,400		$36,400
Outstanding debt	$170,000		

"The bank denied my request citing my poor credit rating and made the following comments on why I would have problems repaying my loan.

1. "I am not living within my means, spending much more than I take in (21 percent), and I have been doing so for years, thus demonstrating my inability to control my expenses.
2. 6–10 percent of my income will be needed just to pay interest on my loans.
3. If I could reduce my expenses by an additional $2,000 a year and use it to pay down my loan, it would take 85 years to complete.

"To put it bluntly, the bank told me my credit rating stinks. Just like Ed Norton said in one of *The Honeymooners* episodes, 'The applicant is a bum.' When I asked the bank to reconsider the loan and lend me $170,000 for thirty years at a rate under 4 percent, they responded with a question: What fool would lend money to someone in your financial condition?

Certainly the bank was justified in turning down Ralph's loan request, because there was a huge chance their loan would not get repaid."

I'm sure it's obvious to the reader that the point I'm getting at is that Ralph's financial stability and the financial stability of the United States are the same. It's just a matter of adding zeros to the numbers and changing the name of some of the expense categories.

Comparing Ralphs and Alice's Expenses to Uncle Sam's

	Expenses		Income	
R & A	College tuition	$9,100	Salary	$30,000
US	Pensions	$**910,000**,000,000	Revenues	$**3,000,000**,000,000
R & A	Medical insurance	$9,700	Loan	$6,400
US	Health care	$**970,000,000**,000	Budget Deficit	$**640,000**,000,000
RK	Private education	$1,100		
US	Education	$**110,000,000**,000		
R & A	Real estate tax	$4,000		
US	Welfare	$400,000,000,000		
R & A	Mortgage payment	$8,200		
US	Defense	$820,000,000,000		
R & A	Home security	$500		
US	(US) Protection	$50,000,000,000		
R & A	(R&A) Transportation	$1,000		
US	(US) Transportation	$100,000,000,000		
R & A	(R&A) Loan Interest	$2,200		
US	(US) Debt Interest	$220,000,000,000		
R & A	(R&A) Other	$600		

US	(US) Other	$60,000,000,000		
R & A	Totals	$36,400	$36,400	
US		$3,640,000,000,000	$3,640,000,000,000	
R & A	Outstanding debt	$170,000		
US	Outstanding debt	$17,000,000,000,000		

Note: *R & A*: Ralph and Alice; *RK*: Ralph Kramden; *US*: US government.

A family of three or four living on an income of $30,000 a year is a difficult undertaking at best, especially when you realize that the average income for an individual in 2013 was $51,000 and that some families have two wage earners. Add to that Ralph's $170,000 in IOUs and the need to borrow more to pay his bills. There's no question that Ralph and Alice have major financial problems.

A town with 1,000 families that was in the same financial situation as the Ralph and Alice would certainly be classified as a poor town. A city with a million similar families or a state with 10 million similar families would both be financial basket cases. Of course this is not the case, as most towns' cities and states have a mixture of low, middle and high income individuals and families.

The balance sheet of the U.S. Government is a different story altogether. Ralph is a poor credit. His credit rating stinks because his income cannot support his expenses, and his debt locks him into a financial black hole from which it will be next to impossible to escape.

Multiplying Ralph's income and expenses by 100 or by 1000 will not improve his ability to meet his obligations or improve his credit rating. It's not the actual numbers that matter, it's the ratios. If his income increased by 10 times and his expenses and debt are also increased by 10 times you are back to square one. No bank or lending institution will lend Ralph a dime whether his income was $30,000 or $30,000,000 a year with these income and expense ratios.

Like I just stated, multiplying Ralph's income and expense ratios by 1,000 or 1,000,000 and you do nothing to improve his credit rating, but multiplying it by 100,000,000 and you're a stellar credit. That's right! A 5 star credit risk. Credit agencies like Moody's and Fitch rate your debt as the safest investment on the planet, closely followed by S & P. As shown above, the income, expense and debt ratios of the U.S. Government are exactly the same as Ralph's, yet investors around the world are willing to lend us trillions of dollars for 30 years at an interest rate of less than 4% and for 10 years at an interest rate of less than 3%.

There are those who would criticize this analysis because I put Ralph in the same category as the US government. They would probably point out that the government has taxing powers and laws that guarantee a revenue stream, and they are correct. What the government doesn't have is individuals' flexibility in cutting expenses—that is, the government has the opportunity to generate income but not the political willpower. Anyway, this argument is not relevant to the issue. The issue is the perception that investors have of the creditworthiness of the United States in spite of its poor balance sheet and huge debt. The major credit agencies perpetuate this fantasy with their top credit ratings. In my opinion, purchasers of US debt will wake up one day and realize that the national debt supports a government whose financial condition is a fantasy and is supported by a house of cards.

When the housing bubble burst around 2008, the major credit agencies were caught off guard. They had given their top AAA rating to many mortgage-backed securities backed by home loans. They believed that the housing market was shielded from violent price changes. In what now seems like the blink of an eye, the housing bubble burst, and on a national level the value of mortgages dropped in value by trillions of dollars. Many AAA-rated bonds quickly became junk bonds. The rating agencies had miscalculated the risk in the underlying asset (the home loans). In my opinion, they are now repeating this mistake in severely overrating the creditworthiness of the United States and its $18 trillion debt.

Rating the Rating Agencies

The major rating agencies (S&P, Moody's, and Fitch) failed miserably when they severely overrated mortgage-backed securities prior to the 2007–2008 recession. What was supposed to be the first line of defense for investors turned out to be a gross misrepresentation of the riskiness of the investments and by extension the true market value of the securities. If these securities were properly rated to reflect the risk of the underlying assets (home loans), it is probable that the housing bubble would have never developed and the entire recession may have been avoided.

Currently Planet Earth consists of over 190 nations. Of these, fewer than twenty earn the top rating of the three major credit-rating agencies. Moody's short definition of a top rated entity is: "Obligations rated AAA are judged to be of the highest quality, with minimal credit risk."

Envision a world with a fictitious country that has an economy equal to that of the United States and has no national debt, no unfunded liabilities, a balanced budget, and a positive economic outlook for years to come. It stands to reason any nation the size of the United States that sported such strong financial numbers would deserve the highest possible rating.

However, the United States as it exists today, in my opinion, sports a balance sheet that would barely qualify it for a rating much higher than junk bond status. The financial condition of the United States looks more like the balance sheet of Greece, Spain, or Italy—the three countries that personify what a poor economy looks like and in recent times caused negative ripples in many of the world's bond and stock markets.

The United States is expected to have a national debt approaching $20 trillion by the time president Obama leaves office. We have not done a very good job on spending, borrowing about $1 trillion a year over the last six years just to meet budget expenses. In addition, by 2017 the United States will need to budget at least $1 trillion a year just to cover debt interest expense. In a normal interest rate environment, at least 20 percent of all tax revenues would be required just to pay the interest on the national debt. This statement assumes an interest rate of at least 5 percent, which is less than the average interest rate over the forty-five years preceding the 2007–2008 recession. Add to that around $90 trillion in unfunded liabilities and perpetual budget overruns, and you have a picture of the United States as it exists today.

In my opinion, the major rating agencies are currently misrepresenting the true value of the Treasury securities that comprise the national debt. Moody's and Fitch currently assign their top rating to the sovereign debt of the United States in spite of all the financial issues I just identified. (S&P assigned the United States the second-highest rating.) Two of the three rating agencies rate the creditworthiness of the United States as perfect, equal to the creditworthiness of the fictitious nation I just described, a nation with a perfect balance sheet.

How the rating agencies justify their ratings is beyond me. I confess that I don't have a clue about the process the rating agencies use to determine the credit status of any entity, but I don't believe that it should in any way distract from my opinions and conclusions. After all, I believe my opinion is just stating the obvious.

Any corporation whose balance sheet listed more liabilities than assets would be considered bankrupt. The rating agencies thus apparently believe that the balance sheet of sovereign nations deserve different considerations than a corporation. This, of course, is correct given that sovereign nations have the power to regulate their income and spending. However, this power is often abused by politicians because spending brings in votes and taxes chases voters away.

There is no question that the United States is far and away the largest economic power on earth. This, of course, raises the question, Why can't the United States live within its means? This is a matter for a separate discussion, but I will point out that we have the added responsibility of being the protector of the free world, which requires an overwhelming and costly military presence. In addition, through the use of foreign aid we attempt to guarantee our sphere of influence.

In my opinion, the best gauge of a country's financial stability is its debt-to-GDP ratio. This represents the total (gross) amount a country borrows as a percentage of its gross domestic product. Though the following stats from the IMF in table 4.11 may be a little dated, they do illustrate my point.

TABLE 4.11.

Country	Stat. date	Debt-to-GDP ratio
United States	February 2014	106%
Italy	June 2012	108%
Spain	April 2013	167%
Greece	June 2011	174%

According to Eurostat, the average debt-to-GDP ratio of the twenty-eight member countries of the European Union was 87 percent (2013). Table 4.12 illustrates this.

TABLE 4.12.

	Public balance (net borrowing/lending of consolidated general government sector)				General government debt (general government consolidated gross debt)			
	2010	2011	2012	2013	2010	2011	2012	2013
EU-28	-6.5	-4.4	-3.9	-3.3	79.9	82.4	85.2	87.1
Euro area (EA-18)	-6.2	-4.1	-3.7	-3.0	85.5	87.4	90.7	92.6
Belgium	-3.8	-3.8	-4.1	-2.6	95.5	99.2	101.1	101.5
Bulgaria	-3.1	-2.0	-0.8	-1.5	16.2	16.3	18.4	18.9
Czech Republic	-4.7	-3.2	-4.2	-1.5	38.4	41.4	45.2	46.0
Denmark	-2.5	-1.9	-3.9	-0.8	42.8	46.4	45.4	44.5
Germany	-4.2	-0.8	0.1	0.0	82.5	80.0	81.0	78.4
Estonia	0.2	1.1	-0.2	-0.2	6.7	6.1	9.8	10.0
Ireland	-30.6	-13.1	-8.2	-7.2	91.2	104.1	117.4	123.7
Greece	-10.9	-9.6	-6.9	-12.7	148.3	170.3	157.2	175.1
Spain	-9.6	-9.6	-10.6	-7.1	61.7	70.5	86.0	93.9
France	-7.0	-5.2	-4.9	-4.3	82.7	85.2	90.6	93.5
Croatia	-5.4	-7.8	-5.0	-4.9	45.0	52.0	55.9	67.1
Italy	-4.5	-3.7	-3.0	-3.0	119.3	120.7	127.0	132.6
Cyprus	-5.3	-6.3	-6.4	-5.4	61.3	71.5	86.6	111.7
Latvia	-8.2	-3.5	-1.3	-1.0	44.5	42.0	40.8	38.1
Lithuania	-7.2	-5.5	-3.2	-2.2	37.8	38.3	40.5	39.4
Luxembourg	-0.8	0.2	0.0	0.1	19.5	18.7	21.7	23.1
Hungary	-4.3	4.3	-2.1	-2.2	82.2	82.1	79.8	79.2
Malta	-3.5	-2.7	-3.3	-2.8	66.0	68.8	70.8	73.0
Netherlands	-5.1	-4.3	-4.1	-2.5	63.4	65.7	71.3	73.5
Austria	-4.5	-2.5	-2.6	-1.5	72.5	73.1	74.4	74.5
Poland	-7.8	-5.1	-3.9	-4.3	54.9	56.2	55.6	57.0
Portugal	-9.8	-4.3	-6.4	-4.9	94.0	108.2	124.1	129.0
Romania	-6.8	-5.5	-3.0	-2.3	30.5	34.7	38.0	38.4
Slovenia	-5.9	-6.4	-4.0	-14.7	38.7	47.1	54.4	71.7
Slovakia	-7.5	-4.8	-4.5	-2.8	41.0	43.6	52.7	55.4
Finland	-2.5	-0.7	-1.8	-2.1	48.8	49.3	53.6	57.0
Sweden	0.3	0.2	-0.6	-1.1	39.4	38.6	38.1	40.6
United Kingdom	-10.0	-7.6	-6.1	-5.8	78.4	84.3	89.1	90.6
Iceland	-10.1	-5.6	-3.8		93.0	99.1	96.4	
Norway	11.1	13.6	13.9	11.1	42.9	27.8	29.1	29.5
Turkey	2.8				42.4			

(*) Data extracted on 23.04.2014

Source: Eurostat (online data codes: tec00127 and tsdde410)

At a 106 percent debt-to-GDP ratio, the financial stability of the United States can only be described as poor. Yet, despite of this glaring black eye, the rating agencies still give the United States a stellar credit rating. Perhaps the rating agencies rate sovereign debt on a curve. They may view the sheer size of our economy as our strongest point and conclude that size alone would be a major factor that will enable us to better withstand major financial shocks. If this is the case, they are absolutely wrong. The bursting of the housing bubble affected every single and multi-family home in the United States. To the best of my knowledge, the fact that the US housing market is the largest in the world had no effect in the way this crisis played out. I believe the rating agencies do view the size of the American economy as a major positive—after all what other reason would they have for issuing their top rating?

I am of the opinion that the end of the Federal Reserve's bond-buying program will bring on a demand by investors for higher interest rates on Treasury securities. The purpose of the extremely low interest rate policy put into effect by the Fed at the start of the 2007–'08 recession was to stimulate the economy. However, in my opinion, even the Fed was unsure of its own ability to keep interest rates at the low levels it had set. The massive debt accumulated during the early stages of the recession had damaged the creditworthiness of United States. In order to keep interest rates down, the Fed undertook an unprecedented action and started a massive bond-buying program, purchasing $75 billion worth of bonds a month. This action, in fact, was an insurance policy undertaken by the Fed to prevent bond traders from pushing interest rates up. Its total purchase exceeded $4 trillion. In my mind, the Fed's purchase only solidifies my belief that without its intervention, interest rates would surely rise and it was aware of this.

The Federal Reserve's bond-buying program ended in October 2014. I believe that soon bond traders will demand higher interest rates before adding to their positions. While the bond-buying program was in effect, bond investors could not do anything to offset the Fed's action, but once the program ended, I believe interest rates will trend upward, possibly sharply upward. The reason for this increase is the deterioration of the financial condition of the United States that has taken place since the start of the recession. The biggest factor being the 80 percent increase in the size of the national debt from $10 trillion to $18 trillion. I also believe that the Wall Street slogan "Don't fight the Fed" will go down in flames and that many traders worldwide will liquidate their investments or hold back on purchasing new investments until they receive higher rates in compensation for the added risk in owning US debt. The Fed will probably appear hapless, as they will be unable to stop it.

As previously stated, if the major rating agencies factored in the size of the US economy in assigning their best or near-best rating, they are severely off base. When it comes to evaluating the creditworthiness of a country whose financial condition is in question, being the biggest is not an asset, it's a liability, because it requires a larger effort for a nation to get it house in order. Additional outside assistance will also be harder to get for a larger country than a smaller country. Compare the assistance needed to bail out Greece to the assistance that will be needed to bail out the United States. The major credit agencies are doing this country and those who invest in our debt a severe disservice in masking the true status of our economic condition and, by extension, masking the risk in investing in Treasury securities that support the national debt.

Because of the Fed's low rate policy, the purchaser of the ten-year Treasury note in 2012 will be stuck with an interest rate of about 1.75 percent, as shown in figure 4.6, which will continue through 2022. If an investor made that same purchase in October of 2015, he or she would be stuck with an interest rate of about 2.1 percent through 2025. If my assumptions are correct, by 2020 the ten-year Treasury will yield between 5 and 7 percent interest. In fact, I believe these securities should yield the higher rates right now. The Fed's low rate policy enforced by its bond-buying program prevented this from taking place. Nevertheless, these Treasury securities will still be overpriced because the major credit agencies will continue to severely overrate the creditworthiness of US debt.

Figure 4.6. Interest rate on the ten-year Treasury note, 2000–2014

As I previously stated, had the major credit-rating agencies properly rated the mortgage-backed securities that were used to finance the overvalued home loans, the housing bubble may have been prevented and the recession avoided. Once the recession began and the finger pointing started, the credit-rating agencies took a lot of heat. You would think that taking the blame for a recession that caused both home owners and stock-holders many trillions of dollars would encourage the agencies to reevaluate their criteria for assigning credit ratings. Since two of the three major credit agencies continue to assign their top credit rating to US debt, I can only presume nothing has changed.

Unfortunately politics always plays a role in major issues unfavorable to a group's ideology. On August 5th of 2011, S&P lowered the rating of US sovereign debt from AAA to $AA+$ with a negative outlook. On August 11th (only four days later), the Democratic Congressional Campaign Committee decided to investigate S&P on the issue of its downgrade. This may be a factor in why the credit-rating agencies continue to overrate US debt.

The major credit agencies blew it once and now they are blowing it again.

In Summary

If the national debt didn't exist, and the government could manage a balanced budget for the next thirty years, that would be great, but the national debt is real and humongous and will continue to grow at an accelerating pace. The only way to reduce it is through a budget surplus, and the only way to freeze it is to balance the budget. Unfortunately the situation is only getting worse. In the last eight years (2008–2015), the budget averaged more than $700 billion in deficits over and above the cost of debt interest. So, taking that together with debt interest, we are talking about budget cuts in the area of $1.5 trillion before a balanced budget can be achieved.

Assigning blame for this crisis would appear relatively easy. Of course Congress's and the president's aggressive spending programs are the main culprits, but the Federal Reserve should share some of the blame. After all, its charter is to fight inflation and keep unemployment down. While it's true the Fed does not have the power of the purse, it does have the power of the pulpit. When it speaks, those in power hang on every word. When the national debt crisis blows up, unemployment will skyrocket, and it will almost certainly have a severe negative effect on inflation. The Fed at a minimum should have been pounding the table, warning Capitol Hill of the risks associated with unbalanced budgets and the ballooning national debt. On this matter it failed miserably.

The political willingness to address this problem is almost nonexistent because it conflicts with politicians' primary agenda, which is to get reelected. They rarely address the issue and usually minimize its seriousness. Their "out of sight, out of mind" strategy has proved to be a stunning success. The majority of citizens don't believe that they spent even one cent in taxes to pay down the national debt and therefore they don't even think about it. Our leadership may keep kicking the can down the road, but they won't be able to keep doing that continuously through 2043.

Of course it's likely that intervention of some sort will take place before the national debt reaches that level. But then again, instead of going forward thirty years, go back thirty years to 1983, when the national debt was $1.4 trillion. I'm sure the same comment would have been made then about the absurdity of an $18 trillion debt in 2015.

While China and Russia awaken to the futility of socialism and the benefits of capitalism, we are stupidly moving in the opposite direction. In my opinion, we are governed by a president with an extreme liberal agenda and a Congress that needs to use a dictionary to find out the meaning of the word *integrity*. I believe the government has locked itself into spending programs that will result in continuous budget deficits as far as the eye can see.

Think about this! It will take more than $1 trillion in new taxes and/or budget cuts to get anywhere near a balanced budget. If, by some miracle, Congress does this, we will still carry annual debt interest of $1 trillion or more into infinity. Unfortunately this is the most positive outcome, and there's zero chance of it happening. The most likely outcome is default and all the ramifications that come with it. It won't bring an end to American exceptionalism, because that is based on our constitutional principles. But it will knock it down a few notches.

Chapter 5: Deficit Spending—Big Time!

The current mindset of the political leadership regarding deficit spending is both sad and astonishing. Up until 1985, our leadership took fiscal responsibility very seriously as evidenced by the low debt-to-GDP ratio of just 35 percent. Today that ratio stands somewhere between 102 and 106 percent. Since then, there has been a seismic shift in the attitude of politicians on government spending. In 1985, when President Ronald Reagan decided that political ideology trumped fiscal responsibility, he increased deficit spending big time in his term in office. He was determined and succeeded in building up the country's military complex and simultaneously cutting taxes. These actions caused a major spike in the amount of debt the nation was carrying in relation to our GDP. President Reagan was elected because of his conservative principles; however in matters of fiscal responsibility he was the Republican version of a big-spending politician, using "deficit spending" to fund his pet projects. This was a game changer that made it acceptable for future politicians to push costly agendas with full knowledge that they could count on deficit spending to fund their projects. In fact, President George W. Bush treated the Iraq War as an off-budget item and President Obama removed the word *limit* from the term *spending limits*.

Troubled Asset Relief Program—TARP

There were two massive spending programs put into effect by the government at the start of the 2008 recession. One was designed to address the threat to the banking system that was caused by the bust of the housing bubble. The second was designed to counter the recession with various stimulus projects. Both were 100 percent dependent on deficit spending and would add the full cost of the program directly to the national debt. The first is the $700 billion Troubled Asset Relief Program, or TARP, signed into law by President George W. Bush in October 2008. The second is the $787 billion American Recovery and Reinvestment Act, or ARRA, signed into law by President Barack Obama in February 2009. ARRA ultimately cost $830 billion.

TARP was originally designed as a $700 billion program to allow the government to buy the troubled assets of major financial institutions. This program was designed to vastly strengthen the financial ratios of these institutions, which would be possible since they would no longer need to include nonperforming assets on their balance sheets. These assets were the bad loans resulting from the bursting of the housing bubble. This program was never carried out as intended. The market was in a "freefall" led by the banking sector saddled by the bad loans just mentioned.

One measurement of any corporation's strength is the amount of losses it can withstand and still survive. Banks in general are highly leveraged institutions. It is common for a bank to have as little as10 percent equity, meaning that if the value of the bank's assets were to decrease by10 percent, its capital would be wiped out and effectively put the bank out of business. This was by design, as banks are viewed as very stable and safe institutions. Most of their profits come from the spread between the interest they receive on loans and the interest they pay on deposits. Most bank assets are in the form of mortgage-backed securities and government securities.

The banking system of the United States was undergoing a major crisis in 2008, and was on the verge of becoming dysfunctional. The first major collapse was of the 158-year-old Wall Street icon Lehman Brothers in the fall of that year. Lehman Brothers was the country's fourth-largest investment bank and the largest bankruptcy in America's history. The firm held over $600 billion in assets (mostly financial) and had twenty-five thousand employees.

It's important to understand that Wall Street is like one big spider-web, where every financial institution in connected at the hip to every other financial institution. Just about every single stock or bond transaction is made with some financial institution acting as the middleman. The Lehman Brothers bankruptcy meant that existing commitments between the company and its Wall Street counterparts were put at risk. Lehman's situation was made more precarious by the probability that just about every major Wall Street institution chose to no longer do new business with the company in order to protect themselves from a potential losses, fearing that Lehman could not make good on its commitments.

Of course it was the financial institutions that were at the center to the storm that caused the stock market meltdown and the subsequent recession, because they were the ones who were heavily invested in mortgage-backed securities. The market value of these securities was quickly going south, exacerbated by the collapse in home prices and the loan defaults caused by borrowers who walked away from their underwater mortgage loans.

It quickly became apparent that some sort of government intervention was needed to stabilize the financial industry. Here the government took the high road at the start of the crisis, but in my opinion before this issue was off the table it found itself in the gutter. The government, led by Treasury Secretary Henry Paulson, did make a concentrated effort to find a way to save Lehman but was unable to find a solution. Also intensely involved in the government's effort to resolve the financial crisis were Federal Reserve Chairman Ben Bernanke and New York Federal Reserve Bank Head Timothy Geithner. I personally followed this situation very closely, and I cannot emphasize strongly enough what a first-rate job these three individuals did in crisis management. Led by Hank Paulson, they were under enormous pressure, working against a clock that was costing investors well in excess of $100 billion a day in stock market and bond market losses. Bear in mind that the bursting of the housing bubble, along with the major declines in stock prices, resulted in a massive 25 percent loss in household wealth, as shown in table in figure 5.1. That's a $15 trillion loss in total wealth.

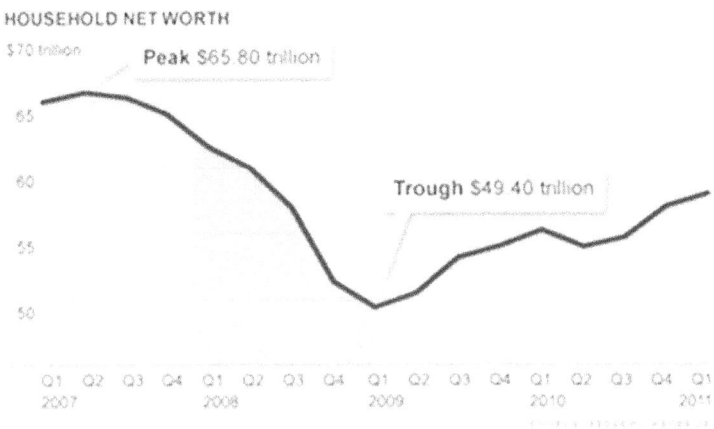

Figure 5.1. Loss of household net worth, 2008 recession.

Two of the three most powerful banks in America, Citibank, and Bank of America, were on the verge of insolvency. Bank of America's stock price fell to less than $4 a share and Citibank's stock price fell to $1 a share. Megafirms Merrill Lynch and Bear Stearns were hemorrhaging capital. They suffered major loan losses on their huge investments in mortgage-backed securities, as shown in figure 5.2. Under Paulson's guidance, both Merrill Lynch and Bear Stearns were sold for a song. Merrill Lynch was sold to Bank of America and Bear Stearns was sold to JPMorgan Chase. As part of TARP, the Federal Reserve guaranteed over $100 billion of the assets of Bank of America and over $300 billion of the assets of Citibank. In addition, speculation also swirled that investment banks Morgan Stanley and Goldman Sachs might also be forced to find larger partners to insure their survival.

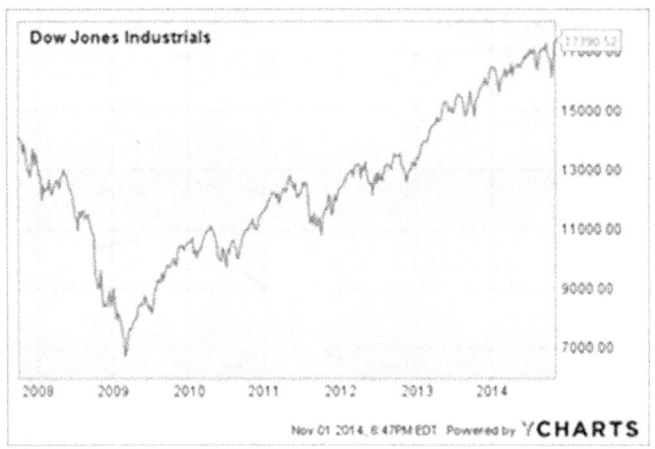

Figure 5.2. Stock market losses, 2008 recession

When the TARP and ARRA programs were put into effect the who's who of Wall Street were on life support and the economy entered a deep recession. Had TARP not been instituted, and had banks the size of Citibank and Bank of America and brokers the size of Merrill Lynch and Bear Stearns been allowed to fail, the effect on the economy would have been catastrophic. The banking system's importance to the economy is equal to an electric company's importance to a city. Would it make sense to let a company such as Con Edison, if they were close to financial insolvency, close shop and shut down the economies of the cities they served? It's not the Con Edison stockholder you're trying to protect. It's the function Con Edison performs in keeping the city running.

Thankfully, Treasury Secretary Hank Paulson recognized the severity of the problem and determined that massive asset purchases from the troubled banks would not suffice and that swifter and stronger action was necessary. So he decided to shore the capital base of the major financial institutions by lending them money. The loans were in the form of preferred stock. This put the government first in line to receive payment if the institution ultimately failed. To Paulson's credit, he would not take no for an answer and even forced the banks who didn't want the loans to accept them. He wanted to make certain that the entire banking system would be viewed as stabilized. TARP also included some assistance for General Motors and Ford. The ten institutions that received the most funds from TARP are shown in table 4.19.

TABLE 4.19. Ten largest recipients of TARP funds

Citigroup	$45.0	GMAC Financial Services	$17.0
Bank fo America	$45.0	General Motors	$13.4
AIG	$40.0	Goldman Sachs	$10.0
JPMorgan	$25.0	Morgan Stanlet	$10.0
Wells Fargo	$25.0	PNC	$7.6

Note: Figures in billions.

In order to raise capital to pay back the government, in 2010 General Motors, AIG, and Citicorp entered the public markets through IPOs (initial public offerings). General Motors raised $18 billion, AIG $20 billion, and Citigroup $10 billion. The program ended in December of 2014 when the government sold the last of its $19 billion stake in Ally Financial. Ally Financial was formally the General Motors Acceptance Corporation, or GMAC, the financial arm of General Motors.

Much to the surprise of the naysayers, TARP proved to be a stunning success. Not only did the program stabilize the banking system; it actually netted a $15 billion profit for the government. The TARP bill had a spending cap of $700 billion, but the government actually used only $426 billion of that amount to shore up the banking system. At the time, the government-started TARP started took a lot of heat because many believed it put Wall Street's interests ahead of Main Street's interests. The fact is that bailing out Wall Street was a prerequisite to helping Main Street. In 2010, in what was in my opinion a knee-jerk reaction, Congress passed a law that banned future bank bailouts as part of the Dodd-Frank bill. Trust me when I tell you that this was a meaningless action. If a similar banking crisis happened again, the government will again step in and bail out the banks, as they will have no choice. The alternative would be disastrous.

TARP's goal was to stabilize the financial industry. Even though the execution of the plan was changed on the fly, it successfully achieved its goal and, amazingly, at no cost to the taxpayer. The government team led by Paulson, Bernanke, and Geithner showed the public how and where it used the TARP funds, the results of its investments, and exactly how the funds were paid back. In fact, I truly believe that Paulson's masterful handling of the crisis should have garnered him a Nobel Prize. I don't believe most people truly understand the pressure he was under and the significance of his accomplishment. It had a major positive effect on just about every economy in the industrialized world.

American Recovery and Reinvestment Act—ARRA

The American Recovery and Reinvestment Act, or ARRA, had problems from the very beginning. Its goals were loosely defined as a government effort to kickstart the economy through various undefined stimulus programs. In my opinion, in order for the program to have been successful, it would have had to do more than just kickstart the economy. It would have had to generate at least as much in tax revenues as the program cost—that is, over the long term it would have had to boost the economy enough to generate $830 billion in tax revenues. Remember that the government got this $830 billion as a loan from the American taxpayer by borrowing it from the national debt. In fact, the ARRA program works out to a loan to the government of $7,200 from each of the 115 million American households.

There were many reports devoted to analyzing the results of this program, but none could estimate the tax revenues the program would generate. The program had many goals, including boosting GDP growth, rebuilding infrastructure, and the like, but it was job creation that topped that list. A study by James Feyrer of Dartmouth College in June of 2012 addressed this issue. Using various economic formulas, he noted that the stimulus program created one job at a cost of between $107,000 and $400,000, and suggested that when all the factors of the stimulus program are included the average cost per job came to about $267,000.

In February 2014, James Freeman in a *Wall Street Journal* column made some noteworthy observations. He suggested that the White House was urged by the influential economist and *New York Times* columnist Paul Krugman to stimulate the economy through a huge government spending program of at least $600 billion. (Bear in mind that only four months earlier, the government approved the $700 billion TARP.) The government met his request and then some, spending about $830 billion. The same liberal economists who enthusiastically supported the plan complained that the reason the plan failed was because it was too small. At the time, the national debt was about $10 trillion. Maybe we should have spent $2 trillion on the program—a trillion hear, a trillion there, no big deal. Wow; here we handed one of the biggest-spending liberal presidents in history a $787 billion gift to dole out as he pleased. A president who in every year of his first seven years in office spent on average more than $1 trillion over and above the tax revenues collected. He, with the blessing of a supportive Congress, in his first seven years in office, increased the national debt by over $7 trillion. As much wasteful spending as there was, apparently $787 billion wasn't enough. The total cost of the program was actually $830 billion. The $43 billion increase for the original plan is just a rounding error in favor of our president.

The plan's main objective was to increase employment, yet unemployment remained over 8 percent for about four more years, right through 2012. Even with the $830 billion in ARRA funds and budget deficits totaling more than $4 trillion, the economy only averaged an anemic 2.4 percent growth rate over that same four-year period.

President Obama pushed the program as an economic savior. Much was said about the need for a huge stimulus program with the assumption that the larger the program, the more effective the program would be in restoring the economy. Next to nothing was said about how the program would be funded, as if its creators expected the tooth fairy to pick up the tab. This program differs from the TARP program in one very important aspect: Tarp funds was money loaned; ARRA funds was money spent. There is no carrying cost for TARP. The ARRA program will cost taxpayers $39 billion a year, every year until the day the national debt blows up. That assumes an average interest rate of 5 percent and equates to every household writing a check to the government for $340 every year.

In my opinion, this program was a national disgrace. Every year we hear about the billions of tax dollars politicians use to gain votes at home by funneling some federal money to fund some pet project, commonly referred to as "pork." This program was a pork feast. Instead of forming a bipartisan committee to formulate a game plan to insure that taxpayers got the most bang for the buck, we handed President Obama a free reign to dole out $787 billion as he pleased. Remember this is a president who has made no secret that he will use every tool at his disposal, and even some not at his disposal, to push his political agenda.

In my opinion the government did a poor job allocating the funds and a poor job accounting for how the funds were spent. Even the Congressional Budget Office (CBO) made the following comments in 2014 in its review on the impact of the program: (1) "[The government's own reports] do not provide a comprehensive estimate of the law's impact on US employment"; (2) "The CBO had issues concerning the quality of the reports' data"; and (3) "The CBO's estimated that close to half of the programs funds were allocated in fiscal year 2010." Which, of course, means that 50 percent of the so- called emergency funds to stimulate the economy were still unallocated over a full year after the program was approved. The CBO also noted that it wasn't until late 2013 before 95 percent of the funds were allocated.

The level of government incompetence on the project is laughable. I think *Saturday Night Live* could have had a field day mocking Washington with this issue. In October 2008, the country was undergoing one of the most severe fiscal crises in its history. A crisis that cost Americans 25 percent of their household wealth and 40 percent of their stock market investments. Hank Paulson successfully identified the need to stabilize the financial industry and successfully implemented the emergency TARP measures, probably the largest bailout program (in term of dollars) in our country's history. Only four months later the government approved an even-bigger emergency program.

Even more problematic are many of the programs that were funded to "quick start" the economy. To add insult to injury, as part of this program, $535 million was invested in Solyndra, the green-energy solar panel manufacturer. In August of 2011, Solyndra went bankrupt and closed shop costing taxpayers all of the government's $535 million investment. Wall Street is loaded with investment bankers who for many decades invested in projects that helped to make America the largest capital creator in the world and the envy of every industrialized country. You would think that the White House would first seek the advice of Wall Street before tossing around billions of taxpayer dollars on pet projects. But, then again, I don't think President Obama could be classified as a supporter of capitalism. Here are some examples of how the funds were invested to quick start the economy:

1. To expand tax credits for college tuition, $14 billion was spent. Here we have taxpayers forking up $14 billion to assist in funding college tuitions. And it was a program that would require one-to-four years before any results could be achieved.
2. In order to deduct sales tax from car purchases, $1.7 billion was invested. It was a program to help one of the president's most loyal political contributors, the auto unions.
3. For Medicaid, $86 billion was spent. But is there even one single Medicaid recipient who would not get aid without this $86 billion having been invested? This simply built up the reserves of the Medicaid program and did not affect the economy at all.
4. To provide extended unemployment benefits, $40 billion was invested. This may win the blue ribbon for the most unproductive use of the program's funds. President Obama pushed unemployment benefits to ninety-nine weeks, and it stayed that way for five years ending in late 2013. Immediately after Congress allowed the ninety-nine-week unemployment benefit program to expire, the monthly number of jobs in the labor force improved sharply.

5. To study why young people consume malt liquor and marijuana, $783,000 was spent. Wow; here is another instance of the government coming through and helping all those unemployed people who couldn't find jobs by studying why young people consume malt liquor and marijuana.

These two massive spending programs illustrate how fast and easy the government can create huge sums of money. Our political leadership views the national debt as a limitless source of funds that can be accessed at will, with little regard as to how the funds will be paid back. With TARP, the funds were repaid in full, plus a little interest to boot. With the ARRA program, some of the funds will be repaid in the form of increased tax revenues from increased economic activity. How much is anybody's guess. The CBO said it was unable to figure it out, due to the government's poor reporting process. In spite of the $830 billion infused into the economy since 2009 from ARRA, the economy has sputtered along at close to a 2 percent growth rate. In my opinion the program was a massive failure.

Our political leadership loves the fact that the national debt is off the radar. Every year going forward, taxpayers will eat the $39 billion it will cost to carry that $830 billion as part of the national debt. There is no political downside in this situation, as taxpayers will not pay ten cents out of pocket. Instead the government will just add the carrying cost to the national budget and the taxpayer will continue to remain oblivious to the entire situation.

Chapter 6: A Delayed Reaction?

Much of what I have written in this book I wrote over the last two years. Among the points I have tried to make are that the national debt is out of control, the Federal Reserve is wrongly keeping interest rates too low, the major credit-rating agencies are rating US government debt too high, and bond investors will soon demand higher interest rates before purchasing treasuries. Today, in October of 2015, I'm more convinced than ever that all of this is still true. So how come none of this has come to pass? I don't have any hard answers, but as always I have plenty of opinions. If my view is anywhere near correct, than the Treasury market must now be in a bubble.

In addition, up to this point I have said nothing about possible solutions to the national debt crisis. That has not been an omission on my part. There is no easy way out of this problem. There isn't even a hard way out. Paying down the debt from budget surpluses is a pipe dream. The $18 trillion dollar national debt locked the country into permanent budget deficits. Even if Washington could come up with a budget that balanced federal income and expenses, it would have to cut an additional $1 trillion (or one thousand billion) from expenses just to make room for the cost of funding the debt interest.

Pressure on the Federal Reserve

The pressure on the Federal Reserve comes from the growth in the national debt since the start of its low interest rate policy. That started in

2007. During this period the national debt rose from $10 trillion to what it is today, $18 trillion. If the Federal Reserve decides to end its low interest rate policy and bring interest rates back to normal, it would cost taxpayers $180 billion for each 1 percent increase in interest rates. That's an increase of 80 percent over this period. If the Federal Reserve pushes the average interest rate up to 5 percent, closer to the fifty-year norm, and keeps rates above 5 percent, taxpayers will be stuck with an $800 billion annual bill just to pay debt interest. Because interest rates are presently so low, the Fed has no ammunition left in the form of rate reductions if it needed to stimulate the economy. So in order for the Fed to restock its arsenal, it will have to raise rates.

In addition, the Fed's primary function is to adjust interest rates in an effort to keep the economy growing at a steady and manageable pace. When the economy gets too hot, it often creates inflationary pressures. The Fed combats this by raising rates. The growth in the national debt since 2007 has created a major obstacle for the Fed, as inflation requires abnormally high interest rates to cool it down. In order to fight inflation, Paul Volcker raised interest rates to 13 percent for three years, 1980 through 1982. In 1980, the national debt was just over $1 trillion. How can the Fed possibly match that interest rate with the $18 trillion national debt this country carries?

The Pressure on the Rating Agencies

The White House and Treasury Department do some arm twisting to pressure the ratings agencies into assigning their top ratings to US debt. The government severely criticized S&P on its downgrade in August of 2011. However, the biggest problem the rating agencies will face is the fallout from their downgrades on world stock and bond markets. Stocks lost 6 percent of their $14 trillion market cap from that downgrade. The last estimate I got on the total value of all bonds traded in the United States was $37 trillion. I was unable to find out how much these bonds were affected by the credit downgrade, if they were affected at all. If the other major credit agencies had dropped their rating of US debt in conjunction with the S&P downgrade, the market losses would have been much more severe. Interest rates would have risen sharply and all bonds from US treasuries down through junk bonds would have suffered major losses, possibly as much as a few trillion dollars' worth. When S&P issued its downgrade, Moody's and Fitch both reaffirmed their highest rating. That action had a major effect on limiting market losses.

Trying to Define a Market Bubble

Is the market for US Treasury securities in a bubble? I believe it is. I will try to explain my logic for making this statement. Unlike corporate stocks, whose price is usually based on growth potential and a possible dividend, bond prices are strictly valued on safety. All other things being equal, the safer the bond the lower the interest rate the bond will pay. The safety factor is strictly based on the financial strength of the entity issuing the security. In the world of bonds with equal maturities, junk bonds have the highest yield because the issuing corporation is usually in some sort of financial difficulty. Then you go up the investment ladder to investment-grade corporate bonds. However, the bonds that pay the lowest interest rates are US Treasury securities since they are backed by the "full faith and credit of the US government" and are therefore considered the safest. There seems to be a difference of opinion here. Who are you going to believe, me or Moody's? I just can't resist some sarcasm.

I define a bubble as a class of investments that for one reason or another are overpriced. The best examples of this were the dot-com boom and bust from 1999 through 2001 and the housing boom and subsequent bust in 2007.

Take a look at the eleven-year graph of the NASDAQ Composite index for the period 1994 to 2005 in figure 6.1. Note the movement in the index between 1999 and 2001, when the composite shot up 3,500 points and then lost it all. That 3,500-point gain created $5 trillion in net worth, only to disappear within the next twelve months. The primary reason for owning these risky technology securities was not the dividend but the potential earnings that may come from investing in an industry in its infancy. You hoped you were investing in a company that was going to be revolutionary and had huge growth potential.

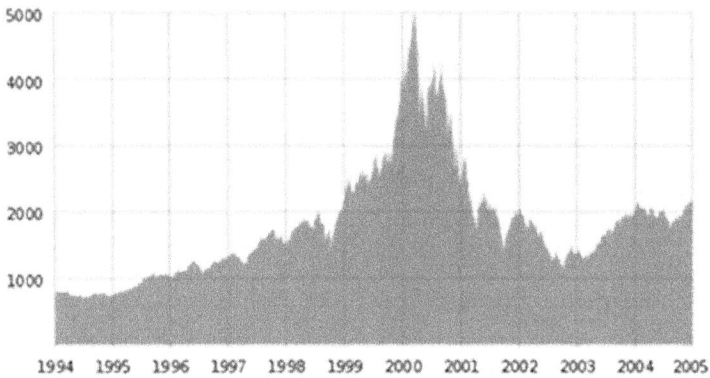

Figure 6.1. NASDAQ Composite index, 1994–2005

How do you know when a class of securities is in a bubble? Obviously you look at the evidence. Take a look at the stock price chart of Cisco Systems in figure 6.2. Note how closely it mirrors the NASDAQ Composite. In one year, the stock price increased from $25 to $75 a share, only to give it all back the following year. Is there anything on this table that would have indicated that when Cisco's stock price was soaring, and that it was in a bubble? I don't see anything indicating as much in this table, or for that matter anywhere else. There certainly were plenty of market gurus raising red flags about the extremely high price-to-earnings ratios, yet in spite of these warnings, investors bid the stock up by 200 percent in less than one year. On the way up, investors believed higher prices were ahead, and on the way down, it was "get out while you still can." It was market sentiment that pushed the NASDAQ up 3,500 points and market sentiment that pushed it back down 3,500 points. The point here is that was no way to really know when the market was in a bubble because there was no evidence to confirm it. That is true for Cisco Systems or for any other of the near-five thousand companies that trade on the NASDAQ, all of which on average lost 80 percent of their value. Only with the benefit of hindsight can you conclude there was in fact a market bubble.

Figure 6.2. Cisco Systems price graph, 1995–2005

There is very little difference between the housing bubble that caused the 2007–'08 recession and the dot-com bubble. The only difference being that the bursting of the housing bubble was a much bigger problem and caused major damage to the entire economy. In both examples, the cause of the bubble was simply the overvaluing of the asset, the dot-com stocks, and the homes. The bursting of the dot-com bubble cost NASDAQ and NYSE investors a total of $6 or $7 trillion. CNN, in a June 2011 post to their website, placed the loss of household wealth resulting from the bursting of the housing bubble at more than $16 trillion. That equates to a 25 percent loss in wealth of the entire country.

Figure 6.3, produced by the Federal Reserve, shows household net worth peaking at $65.8 trillion in 2007 and then falling to $49.4 trillion by 2009. Again, there was no hard evidence that would have shown that either home prices or tech stocks were in a bubble.

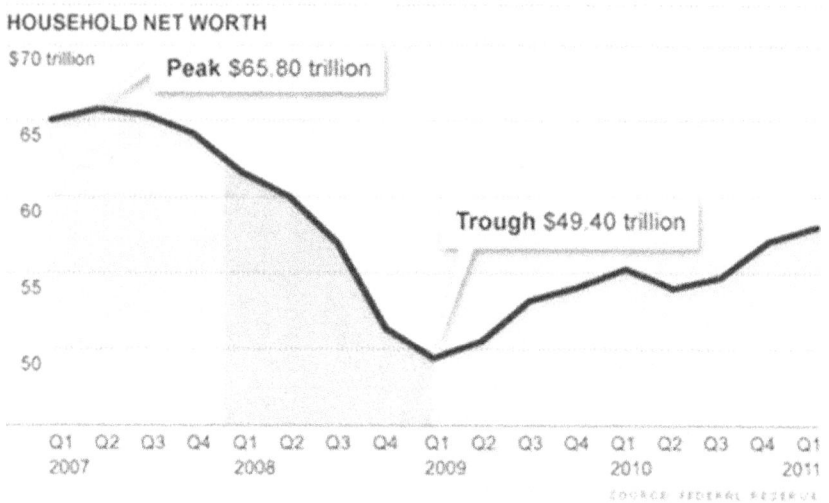

Figure 6.3. Household net worth, 2007–2011

(Note: In the years from 1970 through 2014 [a forty-five-year period], there were forty-one years of budget deficits and only four years of budget surpluses. The surplus years were from 1998 through 2001, the same years as the dot-com boom. You might remember that President Clinton and the Democratic mouthpieces were bragging about the huge amount of jobs created during his administration. They acted as if the tech boom had nothing to do with the creation of jobs and it was the policies of the Clinton administration that were responsible for the strong job market and the budget surpluses achieved during that period. This should put an end to that bogus claim.)

A Bond Market Bubble?

In the case of US treasuries, I have a different view. Here are some of the current factors that lead me to believe that the Treasury market is now in a bubble and has been in bubble territory for quite a while:

- pressure on the major credit-rating agencies by the government to give US treasuries their highest-possible rating
- pressure on the Federal Reserve to keep interest rates at a minimum because of the humongous growth of the national debt and the increased cost of funding it
- the indifference to the national debt crisis by the general public and the media
- the lack of awareness everywhere of the massive cost of funding the national debt when the Federal Reserve normalizes interest rates
- the continuing large budget deficits in spite of the low cost of funding the national debt

In my opinion, the credit agencies are reluctant to downgrade US debt in spite of the country's deteriorating financial condition. I believe the government tried and is still trying to intimidate the credit agencies into keeping their top ratings on US debt.

How the Government Pressures the Credit Agencies

On August 5, 2011, S&P rocked the investment world by lowering the credit rating of US sovereign debt from AAA to its second-highest rating, $AA+$. This was S&P's first downgrade of US debt in its sixty-year history. Since that S&P downgrade, the national debt has risen from $14.5 trillion to about $18.5 trillion. That growth in the debt will increase the severity of losses on world markets resulting from any future downgrades and may be one of the reasons the credit agencies are holding off.

The evidence to support my claim that the government intimidated S&P follows in the actual press release by the agency announcing its downgrade:

August 5th 2011
We have lowered our long-term sovereign credit rating on the United States of America to 'AA+' from 'AAA' and affirmed the 'A-1+' short-term rating.

The downgrade reflects our opinion that the fiscal consolidation plan that Congress and the Administration recently agreed to falls short of what, in our view, would be necessary to stabilize the government's medium-term debt dynamics.

More broadly, the downgrade reflects our view that the effectiveness, stability, and predictability of American policymaking and political institutions have weakened at a time of ongoing fiscal and economic challenges to a degree more than we envisioned when we assigned a negative outlook to the rating on April 18, 2011.

Since then, we have changed our view of the difficulties in bridging the gulf between the political parties over fiscal policy, which makes us pessimistic about the capacity of Congress and the Administration to be able to leverage their agreement this week into a broader fiscal consolidation plan that stabilizes the government's debt dynamics any time soon.

Following are excerpts from news articles that, in my opinion, illustrate pressure and intimidation by the government on the credit agencies:

Reuters:

But Obama administration officials grew increasingly frustrated with the rating agency during the debt limit debate and accused S&P of moving the goal posts in its downgrade warnings, sources familiar with talks between the administration and the agency have said. (Walter Brandimarte and Daniel Bases, August 6, 2011 [the day after the S&P downgrade])

Wall Street Journal:

An angry Timothy Geithner [then secretary of the Treasury] warned the chairman of Standard & Poor's Ratings Services' parent company that the firm would be held accountable for its 2011 downgrade of US debt, a legal filing alleges.

In a phone call with Harold McGraw III [the head of S&P] three days after the downgrade, Mr. Geithner argued that S&P had made an error in its calculations and said the firm's conduct would be "looked at very carefully," according to an affidavit from Mr. McGraw.

The account of the phone call was filed as part of a $5 billion fraud lawsuit brought last year by the Justice Department against S&P.

At the time, the US government and S&P had locked horns on two issues: the debt downgrade and the ratings S&P gave to various mortgage-backed securities prior to the bursting of housing bubble that caused the 2007–'08 recession. The quote continues:

The government alleges that S&P ignored its own standards in assigning credit ratings to mortgage bonds that imploded during the financial crisis, costing investors billions of dollars. The ratings firm, S&P, has long maintained the lawsuit was retaliation for its downgrade of US debt.

S&P's announcement on Aug. 5, 2011, that it was stripping the U.S. of its triple-A debt rating came just days after the government averted a debt-ceiling crisis. The first-ever downgrade of the U.S. roiled world markets and highlighted the impact of political infighting on the economy. The Friday evening decision came after a heated back-and-forth debate between senior Treasury officials and S&P.

"I think S&P has shown really terrible judgment, and they've handled themselves very poorly," Mr. Geithner told CNBC two days after S&P's decision. During that call, Mr. Geithner said the executive and his ratings firm had "done an enormous disservice to yourselves and your country," according to Mr. McGraw's affidavit. [Note: S&P still stands firm on their downgrade as it is still in effect today.]

"The allegation that former Secretary Geithner threatened or took any action to prompt retaliatory government action against S&P is false," a spokeswoman for Geithner, said in an e-mailed statement.

In its request yesterday to U.S. District Judge David Carter for an order that the Justice Department hand over documents for its "retaliation defense," S&P said the government was initially investigating all three major credit rating companies, including Moody's Corp., and focused on S&P exclusively after the McGraw Hill unit downgraded U.S. debt. (Bradley Hope and Damian Paletta, January 21, 2014)

If anything, this confirms the mindset of S&P that the government was intimidating them.

CNNMoney:

Wall Street had its worst day since the 2008 financial crisis, as fearful investors reacted to the United States losing its coveted AAA credit rating. All three major US stock indexes sank between 5% and 7%, pushing the Dow below 11,000 for the first time since last November. Though observers said S&P's downgrade shouldn't matter all that much, the market wasn't buying it. One asset manager was quoted as saying—"Investors are having one reaction to the downgrade: sell first and ask questions later. Those are the factors that led to a drop of more than 6% last week, the worst since the financial crisis of 2008. (A 6 percent drop in the DOW today would be close to 1100 points.)

How to get back to AAA. S&P's downgrade of the United States' credit rating by one notch to "AA+," removed the world's largest economy from the Triple A-club for the first time in history.

Since the rating cut is unprecedented, nobody can be certain what the ultimate impact will be. One thing that concerns investors is the hundreds of downgrades that are coming as a result of S&P's action. The credit agency cut the credit ratings of government-backed mortgage financiers Fannie Mae and Freddie Mac, dozens of U.S. insurance companies, as well as several municipalities that all had AAA ratings before the U.S. downgrade.

In my opinion, this is an example of one of the first things that will happen on the road to Armageddon if all the major rating agencies dropped their ratings to where I believe they should be. It is also a strong factor in understanding why the credit agencies are reluctant to act. The article continues:

> President Obama sought to reassure the public and markets during a midday speech. "The markets continue to reaffirm our credit as among the world's safest," said Obama. "Our challenge is the need to tackle our deficits over the long term. But here's the good news. Our problems are eminently solvable. And we know what we have to do to solve them."

If the president knows what to do, he should make it public and do it! In my opinion, this is pure BS by our president. The article continues:

> With so much uncertainty, investors were leaving little to chance. Despite the downgrade of US debt, Treasury prices rose, pushing yields lower, as investors fled into the relative safety of government-backed debt. (Ken Sweet, August 8, 2011)

How's that for irony? Investors buy government debt to protect themselves from the market gyrations caused by the ratings cut of government debt! This sort of explains why investors accept these very low interest rates. Their mindset is that there is nothing safer than US debt and that it's the best place to put your money while you're riding out a crisis. I wonder if Greek investors felt the same about Greek sovereign debt.

Wall Street Journal:

> A record settlement expected Tuesday between the Justice Department and Standard & Poor's Ratings Services came together over two days in mid-January when the two sides agreed to move past a feud triggered by a surprise down-grade of US debt, according to people familiar with the talks.
>
> In the span of about 30 hours, the Justice Department lowered its asking price and backed off demands that S&P admit to violating laws when it issued rosy grades on risky mortgage deals, the people said. Doing so would have left the ratings firm vulnerable to future lawsuits. S&P, meanwhile, agreed to raise its offer above a key threshold and withdraw its assertion that the Justice Department lawsuit was political retaliation for the ratings firm's 2011 downgrade, the people said.

You can see here, the very threat of losing any lawsuit would bring on the possibility of an avalanche of future class action lawsuits.

> Investors rely on ratings from S&P, Moody's Investors Service and Fitch Ratings when deciding whether to buy bonds. The three issue about 95% of credit ratings globally. (Timothy W. Martin and Andrew Grossman, February 2, 2015)

One of my pet peeves comes into play here. I have been arguing for years that the banks were not at fault for the overpriced mortgage-backed securities that were blamed for the 2007–'08 recession. In my opinion, the banks were doing business as usual, and the crisis was strictly the result of the collapse in home prices. In addition, it was the government that put pressure on the banks to lend with loose standards. If you think I'm all wet on this issue, please read this March 9, 2015, *Wall Street Journal* lead editorial:

Bloomberg:

> In his court statement, McGraw, 65, said Geithner called him on Aug. 8, 2011, after S&P was the only credit ratings company to downgrade the U.S. debt. Geithner, McGraw said, told him that S&P would be held accountable for the downgrade. Government officials have said the downgrade was based on an error by S&P.
>
> "S&P's conduct would be looked at very carefully," Geithner told McGraw according to the filing. "Such behavior would not occur, he said, without a response from the government." (Edvard Pettersson, January 21, 2014)

There's more articles on the subject, but these are sufficient to make the point. Since S&P issued its downgrade in August of 2011, the national debt increased by $3.5 trillion, to the current $18 trillion. What's another $3.5 trillion? That's $300 billion more than all the income tax revenues collected from both individuals and corporations in 2014. Yet, in spite of an $18 trillion national debt, the rating agencies remain stringent and continue to stand by their top ratings. In my opinion, the ratings agencies are holding off on a downgrade for at least two reasons: First, I believe they are feeling immense pressure from the government, as was shown in the government's reaction to the 2011 downgrade by S&P, and next, I believe they are in fear of the enormous consequences a downgrade would have on the financial markets throughout the world. In addition. any meaningful downgrade will also result in a chain reaction of downgrades of lesser-quality bonds. Bear in mind that a downgrade of only one notch by one major credit agency (S&P) caused a drop equal to 1,100 points in today's market.

The Mindset of the Investor

I think the investor's mindset is the most difficult area to address, because ultimately it is the investor who has the final say on what interest rates he or she will accept before purchasing US debt. I believe this statement is logical; however, in my opinion bond investors are acting like a bunch of lemmings. They act as if they are totally ignorant of the poor financial condition of the country and accept the ratings the credit agencies issue as the gospel. They also accept whatever interest rate the Federal Reserve deems appropriate to the current economic conditions, rarely buying or selling treasuries more than half a point away from the Fed's benchmark rate. You would expect the investor to assess the credit-worthiness of the entity he or she is investing in and then demand whatever interest rate is appropriate to the riskiness of the security. So much for logic. In January of 2000, the ten-year Treasury bond yielded 6.6 percent and the national debt was under $6 trillion. Today the national debt has more than tripled to $18.5 trillion and the ten-year bond yields under 2 percent. What's wrong with this picture?

I previously stated that the slogan "Don't fight the Fed" was doomed to go down in flames as investors wake up to the weak financial condition of this country. I may have to rethink that opinion.

If memory serves me correctly, prior to the Ben Bernanke era, the Fed usually kept its opinion on where interest rates should be to itself. The only time rate moves were predictable was when the economy was in a major expansion or recession. The rest of the time the rate change announcements would be done without warning. When Bernanke took over, he changed Fed policy and started issuing status report-type statements of when future rate changes would occur. The status reports often specified benchmark targets such as preferred inflation rate or a preferred unemployment rate. Prior to the Bernanke era, both bond traders and the Fed moved interest rates around. It was not uncommon for the Fed to move its benchmark rates just to bring them into line with the current market, because bond traders had different ideas of where interest rates should be. As I just stated, bond investors seem more reluctant to challenge the Fed and are willing to accept whatever rate the Fed deems appropriate. The massive bond-buying program of recent years punished investors who thought rates were too low given the country's deteriorating financial condition.

The investor, as well as the general public, remains oblivious to the growth in the national debt. Whether the debt is $3 trillion or $30 trillion, most citizens care very little about it. Only conservatives (myself included) believe this to be a serious problem. The only thing that's going to wake up the general public is the huge interest expense that will come from the continuing growth of the debt, rising interest rates, and/or a downgrade by the major credit agencies. Apparently investors don't care that the United States is up to its eyeballs in debt, and that it won't be too long before debt interest exceeds $1 trillion annually.

Let's go back to 1995 when the national debt was under $6 trillion. That same year, the interest paid on the debt was about $330 billion. Now the national debt has tripled to more than $18 trillion. If interest rates were the same today as they were in 1995, the interest on the current debt would be about $1 trillion. The Cato Institute put the amount of debt interest in 2014 at only $229 billion. This reason that amount seems low is that current interest rates are less than 25 percent of what they were in 1995. Here I have to repeat a very important paragraph that appeared earlier in this book.

My explanation of growing the debt without pain: The national debt grew by about 80 percent, to more than $18 trillion by 2015, from about $10 trillion in 2008. The Fed's low interest rate policy was in effect throughout the period, yet the amount of debt interest paid barely budged from year to year. This was made possible by the fact that debt issued prior to the Fed's low-rate policy yielded higher rates, and upon maturity was rolled over (reissued) at the current low rates. This had the effect of keeping the growth of the national debt out of the public eye, as the government was able to increase the size of the national debt massively without having to increase a comparable amount of debt interest.

Discussing the Federal Reserve

As I previously pointed out, the amount of interest on the national debt in 2014 was $229 billion. That equates to an overall interest rate on the entire national debt of just 1.3. The ultralow rate policy in effect since the start of the 2008 recession is more than likely the longest sustained "zero" interest rate policy in the Fed's history. I say this because just like the rating agencies, the Federal Reserve is under a tremendous amount of pressure. The pressure comes from the government wanting the Fed to keep rates low because low interest rates help the economy. In my opinion, it is likely that President Obama made his position on rates clear to Janet Yellen before appointing her head of the Federal Reserve.

A second and more important point is the impact of normalizing interest rates on the growth of the debt. The pressure on the Fed is the $180 billion it will cost taxpayers for each one-point increase in interest rates. If the Fed wanted to normalize rates and raise the interest rate four points, from 1.3 percent to 5.3 percent, that 4 percent point increase would cost taxpayers an additional mind-blowing $720 billion. The average rate over the last fifty years was at least 6 percent. If that 4 percent jump in rates were to happen in 2016, it would blow up the budget and increase the budget deficit to over $1.2 trillion. Of course, that much of a rate hike would have to be spread out over three or four years. Unfortunately, the budget deficits from each of those three or four years will need to be added onto the national debt. Budget deficits in excess of $1 trillion will be the norm by then.

So you can see the potential havoc raising rates will have on taxpayers and the economy and why the Fed will keep rates as low as possible if it can. The normal interest rate of 5 percent had a purpose. At 5 percent, the Fed had room to maneuver, because when recessionary pressure became apparent, the reduction in rates would serve as a valuable stimulus. At 1.3 percent, the Fed does not have this room. Bear in mind that when the overall rate is that low, short term rates are already at zero.

The rapid growth of the national debt adds another problem. It severely hampers the Fed's ability to fight inflation. When Paul Volcker led the

Fed, he was faced with runaway inflation due the worldwide oil shortage. He pushed interest rates to an average of 13 percent from 1980 through 1982. At that time the national debt was just over $1 trillion. Now with an $18 trillion debt, debt interest alone would add another $500 billion to the budget for each of the three years. That's over and above to $720 billion increase from returning to normal rates.

Another small part the Fed plays in keeping interest rates down is the bonds it accumulated as part of their quantitative-easing program. The Fed bought up over $4 trillion in bonds, $2.4 trillion in treasuries, and the rest in mortgage-backed securities. It's likely that if the market had to absorb these $4 trillion in bonds, interest rates might be a little higher.

Janet Yellen, the Chair of the Federal Reserve

I know nothing about Janet Yellen's personal life and have no reason to think she is anything other than a fine person. I cannot speak to her qualifications to lead the Federal Reserve, as my only expertise in this field is self-taught. My concern is that she may be reluctant to raise rates for political reasons. Please don't give much weight to this analysis because I am well aware my evidence is scant, but it nevertheless it may be a factor in why the Fed. in my opinion. appears overly reluctant to raise interest rates.

On November 6, 2006, Ms. Yellen, then the head of the San Francisco branch of the Federal Reserve Bank, spoke at the University of California, Irvine, on the subject of economic inequality. In my opinion, this subject matter all by itself shows her political bias. I believe that none of president Obama's appointees are allowed opinions that are different from his own. I may be a little naive on this subject, but I believe presidential appointees should be given to people best qualified to fill the position regardless of race or gender. Presidents Obama's method for filling cabinet positions is based on who is best qualified to carry out his political agenda, without question. My problem with Ms. Yellen is that she may be more loyal to President Obama than to our country and, as a result, she may try her best to please the president at the expense of doing what is best for the country.

The Federal Reserve's chairmanship is more than just a cabinet position. The Fed is an independent agency responsible for fighting inflation while targeting full employment. Many times, the Federal Reserve will be required to adjust interest rates in a manner that is contrary to the political goals of Congress and the president. Its independence is essential in order to perform its function.

President Barack Hussein Obama

President Obama campaigned on the promise to fundamentally change America. I don't know if growing the national debt was intentional on his part, but if the national debt crisis blew up during his presidency (and heaven forbid his control of Congress), just think what an opportunity it would have been for him to remake America in the way he thinks it should be. The president and his appointees live by the motto "Never waist a crisis," and if the national debt crisis blows up, the president would have a field day. There is no question in my mind that the president will do almost anything to help himself achieve his ultraliberal philosophy, as was demonstrated by the twenty-plus times he admittedly lied about Obamacare (e.g., you can keep your insurance, your doctor and save $2,500). He made these statements with the conviction of the Pope, and he is on record as lying numerous times on other issues as well.

On July 3, 2008, while candidate Barack Obama was campaigning for president, he made the following statement with regard to the national debt. I think he made this statement in the Senate chambers. It appears he's lost without a teleprompter. He speaks worse than I do!

> The problem is, is that the way Bush has done it over the last eight years is to take out a credit card from the Bank of China in the name of our children, driving up our national debt from $5 trillion dollars for the first 42 presidents—number 43 added $4 trillion dollars by his lonesome, so that we now have over $9 trillion dollars of debt that we are going to have to pay

back—$30,000 for every man, woman and child. That's irresponsible. It's unpatriotic.

In my opinion, President Obama stole the election for his second term as president. Had he told the truth about Obamacare, he never would have been reelected. He now abuses his power and uses executive action to change laws, create new ones, or completely disregard existing ones in order to advance his ultraliberal political agenda. The national debt problem is out of control and I don't think we can look to President Obama for any help in this area. Remember his comment after the S&P downgrade in August of 2011: "But here's the good news. Our problems are eminently solvable. And we know what we have to do to solve them."? He wouldn't lie about this, would he?

Where Are We Headed?

As I previously said, there are four major players that had a role in creating the national debt crisis and will have a role in determining how the crisis plays out regardless of the ultimate outcome. They are the government, the Federal Reserve, the major credit-rating agencies, and the investor. I already spelled out the importance of each player and what its part is in relation to the national debt. Here I will attempt to show how the national debt crisis will play out. The question is not if but when the national debt will blow up. When that happens, it will cause a major economic crisis in the United States and probably the entire free world.

As the national debt grows, the major cause of that growth will shift from deficit spending to the mandatory interest expense of funding the debt. When interest rates normalize, debt interest funding will be the largest expense in the budget, and that expense will increase at a faster rate than any other item in the budget. In other words the biggest reason for the growth of the national debt is the national debt itself.

Need more proof? In the last twenty-one years, from 1994 through 2014, the government budgeted $5.5 trillion just to pay debt interest. That entire $5.5 trillion is now part of the national debt.

The Best-Case Scenario

It all comes down to the mindset of the investor. Remember the S&P downgrade in August of 2011? That downgrade rocked the stock market, yet in spite of it investors ran to, what they believed, was the safety of US government bonds. If there ever was a demonstration of the mindset of the investor, that was it. They ran to US Treasury securities as a safe haven from the turbulence in world markets caused by the downgrade of these very same securities by S&P.

This is pure speculation on my part, but if memory serves me correctly, prior to the Ben Bernanke era, bond investors would have reacted differently—that is, bond values would have also taken a hit, because of the S&P downgrade, believing the downgrade was a direct hit to the creditworthiness of the United States. But, I think these days bond investors have a different view on the safety of US Treasury securities. I think they believe the Federal Reserve has their back and will insure the safety of Treasury securities by stepping in and purchasing US debt when bond investors become reluctant to do so. The $4 trillion bond-buying program that the Federal Reserve undertook to insure that their low interest rate policy would not be challenged by bond investors adds a lot of credibility to this theory. That action by the Fed punished investors who were pessimistic on US debt and kept interest rates at record-low levels. This shill game by the Fed created what I believe is overconfidence in US debt. This overconfidence, in my opinion, is not based on the investor's faith in the strong creditworthiness of the United States but rather the belief that the Federal Reserve would again step up and purchase more bonds to force rates down and again punish investors who are pessimistic on the quality of US debt.

I previously stated that it would ultimately be the bond investor who will bring the national debt problem to a head by backing off from purchasing Treasury securities because of the rotting financial condition of the United States. The need for the Federal Reserve to entice bond investors by boosting interest rates, along with the growth of the national debt, will ultimately require such huge annual debt interest payments that it will become impossible to continue funding the debt. This will be accompanied by a series of debt downgrades by the major credit agencies and ultimately lead to a restructuring of the debt and a partial default by the US government. This action will mean economic Armageddon for the United States, bringing on a crisis that is beyond my imagination. (I discussed some of the possible consequences of a default elsewhere in this book.) I also explained why growing our way out of the debt problem was just a fantasy and that the growth in the national debt far outpaced the growth in the economy.

Option No. 1: The Balanced Budget Option

As I see it, there is only one possible method of avoiding a disastrous outcome. The method is both simple and obvious, but it is also very painful and almost next to impossible to execute. The answer is simply a balanced budget—that is, balanced to the point that it will freeze the growth of the national debt. The goal being that with the national debt frozen at a fixed amount, its significance will diminish over time as the economy grows. Just for the record, in the six years of the Obama presidency to date, the economy grew at an average rate of less than 2 percent. During that same period, deficit spending exceeded 30 percent of the budget. Put another way, budget deficits over that six-year period were close to all the income collected in taxes for two full years.

In theory, if the amount budgeted for debt interest remained constant, then any revenue growth could be used to expand existing programs. In order to achieve a balanced budget, Congress must go through the painful process of cutting ongoing programs or increasing taxes. Over the last two years, budget deficits averaged about $500 billion a year. According to the CBO, the budget deficit for the first half of 2015 was $430 billion. If you use 2016 as an example, we would be talking about budget cuts in the range of $500–$600 billion.

As disagreeable as these suggestions are, the most painful action may be the need to cut spending even more to offset any interest rate increases sure to come when the Federal Reserve starts to normalize interest rates. At the present time, the Fed has set rates at or near-record lows, averaging just 1.3 percent in 2014. It's a certainty that the government will not take any action on balancing the budget during the Obama presidency, and it's equally certain that by the time President Obama leaves office, the national debt will be at or near $20 trillion. Therefore the normalization of interest rates will require a budget allocation of $140 billion–$200 billion for every one-point hike in interest rates. Let's assume that the Fed wants to normalize interest rates at just 4 percent. That will increase debt interest from the current $230 billion to maximum of $800 billion. As rate increases take time to work their way through the system, within three years the government will need to cut the budget by an additional $300–$400 billion. Rate increases will affect 40 percent of the national debt in year one, 55 percent in year two, and 70 percent in year three. Bear in mind that over the last fifty years, the average interest rate on US debt was over 6 percent, and if the Fed chooses to take that path it will add an additional $280–$400 billion in debt interest.

Time is not on the side of the government. The longer it delays taking action, the larger the debt burden will be. The growing debt burden means that a larger-and-larger portion of the budget will be devoted to funding the debt at the expense of ongoing discretionary and nondiscretionary programs.

I hate spouting all this gloom and doom, but the national debt problem cannot be resolved until all the facts surrounding the problem are brought to light. In my opinion, the percentage of the population that truly understands the complexities of the national debt crisis and all the potential problems it will eventually cause is miniscule.

To offset the effect of the expected interest rate hikes by the Federal Reserve, the actions I just described will require at least $500 billion in budget cuts out of the gate, with major additional budget cuts, possibly totaling more than $1 trillion. The possibility of our government going down this road is next to nil.

Option No. 2: Business as Usual

I call option number two "the business as usual option" because there really is no option number two. Business as usual translates into doing nothing. Doing nothing is a sure road to financial Armageddon. Doing nothing will force the government to eventually default. According to a government website, in 2014 the US government had $500 billion more in expenses than it received in revenues—thus a $500 billion dollar budget deficit. Can you, in your wildest imagination, envision our politically sensitive senators and congressmen approving $500 billion in budget cuts? That's a 16 percent cut. You might remember back in 2013 Congress was forced to cut the budget by $85 billion, or about 4 percent, and they cried foul about that.

Who Gets Hurt in a Government Default

At last count, there were about 145 million working Americans. That works out to an IOU to the government of about $127,000 per working individual. If you include the 38 million people collecting Social Security, it works out to just under $100,000 per individual. So who would get hurt by a government default? Who would eat the loss?

The answer would appear to be simple: the investor who owns the treasuries at the time the government defaults will wind up eating the loss. If the government goes down the "default" road, it will not be because it wants to; it will be because it has to. It will be the result of the country's deteriorating financial condition—a condition brought on by never-ending budget deficits, rising and out-of-control interest rates. and a ballooning national debt. The ballooning debt will be caused mostly by the government's policy of borrowing from the national debt to pay the interest needed to fund the national debt.

Simple answer, but that's not the way the debt crisis will actually play out. While it's impossible to forecast how fast this crisis will develop, it will certainly become apparent as interest rates rise to unstainable levels.

Know this: No matter how high interest rates go, and no matter how low Treasury prices fall, there will always be a market for Treasury securities. Someone will always find a way to make money. If Treasury prices fall to 50 cents on the dollar, there will always be someone willing to buy them for 49 cents.

It is difficult to ascertain how the general public will be affected by a default. According to a 2012 Federal Reserve analysis of the ownership of the national debt, only 8.4 percent of the debt was owned by individuals and nonprofit organizations. Nevertheless, that 8.4 percent accounted for more than $1.5 trillion of the national debt. Money market mutual funds and private pension funds each accounted for about $750 billion. Both would take severe hits, as most of the assets that back up these funds are in the form of Treasury securities. State and local pension funds own over $300 billion of the debt, meaning a default will severely hurt their ability to pay the pension benefits to their retirees. Banks and credit unions (US-chartered depository institutions) own over $350 billion, and life insurance companies own about $275 billion of the debt. A massive write-off of US debt in both of these industries would threaten their ability to survive as independent institutions.

The Federal Reserve Bank owns a massive $2.67 trillion of the debt; most of which was accumulated as part of its quantitative-easing (low interest rate) program. A check of the Fed's balance sheet shows that the ownership of these securities is funded by bank reserves and currency in circulation. How a US default will impact the Federal Reserve's ability to function is beyond me. I have to leave it to economic experts to figure it out. However, the largest portion of the national debt is owned by foreign nations, which account for 48 percent of the debt, or $8.8 trillion. China and Japan each own about $1.2 trillion of it. You can be sure a US debt default will rattle world stock and bond markets.

The following figures itemize the breakdown of the ownership of the national debt. The percentage amount of each category is based on the 2012 debt. The dollar amount is based on the 2015 national debt.

TABLE 6.1.

Value of Securities Held By Ownership Type.
$18,300,000,000,000 National Debt

Owner of Securities	Percent of National debt	Dollar Amount if applied to Current National Debt of
Foreign nations	48.40%	$8,857,200,000,000
Federal Reserve	14.60%	$2,671,800,000,000
Households and nonprofit organizations	8.40%	$1,537,200,000,000
State and local governments excl. employee retirement funds	4.40%	$805,200,000,000
Money market mutual funds	4.10%	$750,300,000,000
Private pension funds	4.10%	$750,300,000,000
Mutual funds	3.80%	$695,400,000,000
U.S. chartered depository institutions	2.00%	$366,000,000,000
Security brokers and dealers	1.70%	$311,100,000,000
State and local governments employee retirement funds	1.70%	$311,100,000,000
Life insurance companies	1.50%	$274,500,000,000
Federal government retirement funds	1.40%	$256,200,000,000
Property casualty insurance companies	0.80%	$146,400,000,000
Foreign banking offices in the U.S.	0.70%	$128,100,000,000
Exchange traded funds	0.60%	$109,800,000,000
Nonfinancial corporate business	0.50%	$91,500,000,000
Government sponsored enterprises	0.50%	$91,500,000,000
Nonfinancial noncorporate business	0.40%	$73,200,000,000
Issuers of asset backed securities	0.20%	$36,600,000,000
Credit unions	0.20%	$36,600,000,000
Closed end funds	0.00%	$0
Total	100.00%	$18,300,000,000,000

Percentage of national debt based on the 2013 3rd quarted figure of $11.3 trillion.
Web Site - Global Macro Monitor macromon.wordpress.com
Chart Source - www.ritholtz.com - by Barry Ritholtz
Data Source - Federal Reserve, Flow of Funds

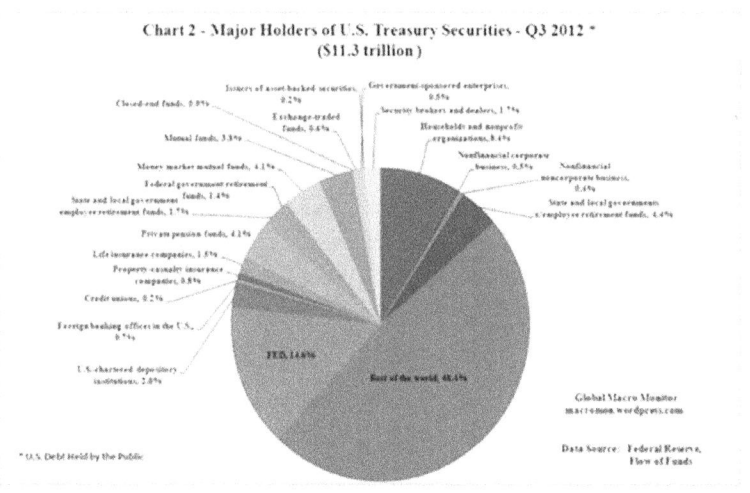

Figure 6.4.

TABLE 6.2.

Major Foreign Holders of Treasury Securities
April 2015

China	1263.4
Japan	1215.7
Caribbean Banking Centers	295.5
Oil Exporting Nations	292.9
Brazil	262.7
Belgium	228.9
Switzerland	215.8
Ireland	215.7
United Kingdom	194.8
Hong Kong	183.1
All Others	1768.8
In Billions Total	6137.3

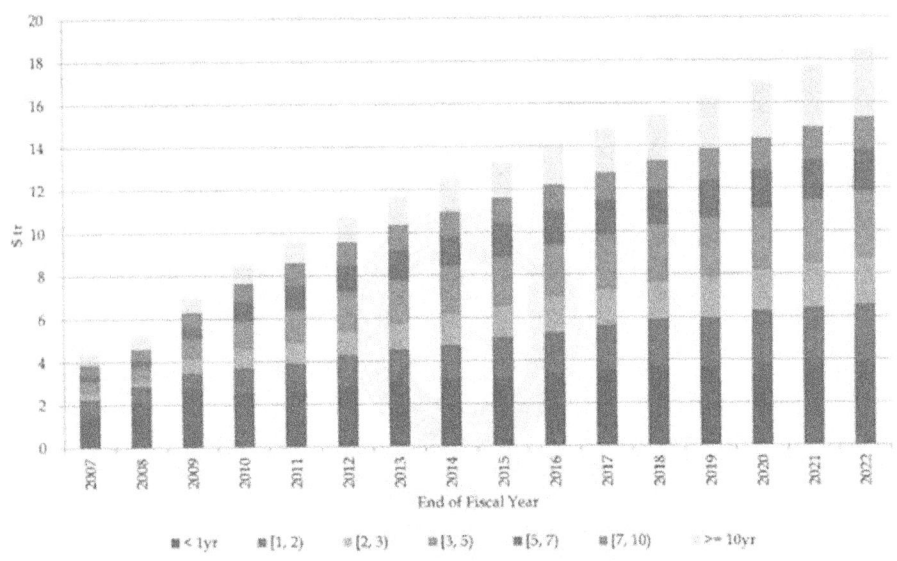

Figure 6.5. The Treasury securities that comprise the national debt (2012) by maturity class.

As I previously suggested, investors backing off the purchase of treasuries will bring the national debt issue to a head. That may happen when
investors grow nervous about the credit quality of US debt, or it may follow credit downgrades by the major credit agencies. Either way, it will
push interest rates higher and reduce the market value of existing Treasury
securities. The Federal Reserve may try to mitigate the crisis by instituting
a massive bond-buying program similar to the $4 trillion stimulus pro-
gram that ended in 2014. That action may initially prove successful since
the Fed packs a powerful punch. But ultimately it will fail. In fact, any
attempt by the Fed in this area will probably backfire and create a crisis
of its own, as the action will appear desperate. In any case, higher interest rates will create ever-higher budget deficits, lower bond values, and a
ballooning national debt. At this point, the national debt crisis will feed
on itself until it reaches the breaking point. When and if that happens, the
government will have no choice but to legislate a partial default on many
Treasury securities. Needless to say, the nation's economy and stock and
bond markets throughout the world will deteriorate into total chaos. This
will be similar to what Greece did, paying owners of its sovereign debt
only 50 cents on the dollar. The act of defaulting on US debt will not unto
itself bring on an economic Armageddon, because that event will have
preceded the default.

I have frequently mentioned what effect the return to normal interest
rates will have on the budget, requiring Congress to allocate at least $1
trillion every year just to meet the interest obligations needed to fund the
debt. That figure will be more than 25 percent of the current budget and
probably 30 percent of government revenues. That means that when the
Fed fully normalizes interest rates, 30 percent of every tax dollar collected
will go to servicing the debt, with that 30 percent being siphoned off and
providing no benefits to our citizens. In the next ten years, taxpayers will
fork up well over $10 trillion just to fund the debt. As 48 percent of the
national debt is owned by foreign countries, that means over the next ten
years US taxpayers will be paying foreign investors at least $4.8 trillion.

With all that said, where's the outcry? Why isn't the public up in arms
about this situation? The reason, in my opinion, is that the vast majority

of the media and the press are in President Obama's camp and support a big spending, ultraliberal agenda. Many politicians, both Democrats and moderate Republicans, also remain silent. The Democrats because they support the president's program, and the moderate Republicans (RINO's) because they will need to spend if and when they come to power. To this day, nothing has changed with regard to government spending, in spite of the drubbing the republicans gave the Democrats in the 2014 elections.

I wish I could quote all those politicians, economists, and op-ed writers who are on record saying the national debt is manageable. I see these people as either uninformed, stupid, or having sold their soul for political reasons.

How High Is Too High?

How much can the national debt grow before investors start to back off, believing Treasury securities are too risky? It's a matter of mindset. At the present time, investors appear to be very comfortable with the credit ratings provided by the major credit agencies and equally comfortable accepting whatever interest rates the Federal Reserve deems appropriate according to its view of the country's economic condition. I envision we will reach a national debt of $100 trillion, $200 trillion, or more, before investor's rebel, in fear that the United States is carrying too much debt. It's more of a question of how fast the debt grows than how high it grows. If the national debt were to grow at the same rate as the economy, carrying the debt load would be a much less of a problem. Remember that from 1984 to the present, the national debt grew by over 1,000 percent, from less than $1.6 trillion to 18.2 trillion, and if that same growth rate persisted for the next thirty years, the national debt would grow to about $180 trillion. That this fact is not a matter of concern to investors, the media, or our political leaders I believe is stark proof that our political leaders, with the support of the liberal press, has achieved a major brainwashing victory, in convincing the public that our massive debt load is not a serious problem. This is a major concern of mine, especially considering the fact that the debt has just about doubled in size over the last seven years. The debt growth has averaged over $1 trillion a year every year President Obama held office. As I previously said, over the last seven years, GDP growth averaged about 2 percent a year; during that same seven-year period the national debt grew by 80 percent, or just under 15 percent a year. Neither the size of the debt nor the speed at which it grew seemed to phase the investor or the credit agencies. In my opinion, as long as the credit agencies continue to give US debt their top or near-top ratings, investors will not balk about the risk in investing in US treasuries, regardless of the size of the national debt, or the interest rates set by the Federal Reserve.

The Path of Least Resistance

On April 14, 2015, the House of Representatives approved a bill that would increase Medicare compensation to doctors, at a cost of $214 billion to taxpayers. The law prevented a 21 percent cut in doctors' fees that was about to go into effect. Two-thirds of the $214 billion needed to finance the bill will come from deficit spending. That one bill will add $140 billion to the national debt. That equates to an IOU to the government of about $1,000 for every working American. The day before the bill was passed, the Treasury Department said that for the first six months of fiscal year 2015 it ran a deficit of $439 billion, bragging that this was a 6 percent cut from the previous year. At about that same time, Fitch ratings affirmed its *AAA* rating of US debt. Fitch added the following one-sentence comment: "The U.S. has achieved a rapid fiscal consolidation based on economic recovery and tight spending limits, but further deficit narrowing will be more hard-won." In my opinion, this is a sick joke. Here we have the government bragging about a budget deficit of $439 billion six months into the fiscal year, and we have one of the major credit agencies reaffirming its *AAA* rating while complementing Congress on its fiscal discipline. This is another stark illustration of Congress using the national debt as the path of least resistance. The path that is greased, in my opinion, by the bogus top ratings issued by the credit agencies.

The more I think about it, the more secure I am in my opinions on the subject of the national debt. I believe the government will not address this crisis until it's forced to buy out-of-control interest rates. This will be the result of investors backing off from buying US treasuries because of the nation's deteriorating economic condition. I believe the major credit agencies are intimated into giving US debt their highest rating. This may be in fear of government reprisals, similar to the events S&P underwent after its 2011 downgrade of US debt. Or it may possibly be the result of the fear the credit agencies had that their downgrades would roil world economies and world stock and bond markets. I believe the Federal Reserve is keeping interest rates artificially low because the huge increase in the size of the national debt will make it next to impossible for the government to meet the interest requirements that can only be paid from tax increases or budget deficits. I believe President Obama could not care less about the national debt and will spend whatever it takes to achieve his ultraliberal agenda. I believe outside of a small conservative minority, both the Senate and the House of Representatives will do nothing about the national debt except give it some lip service.

The remainder of this paragraph appeared earlier in this book, and I think it's appropriate to repeat it again here: Assigning blame for this crisis would appear relatively easy. Of course the aggressive spending programs by Congress and all the presidents since Ronald Reagan are the main culprits, but the Federal Reserve should share some of the blame. Its charter is to fight inflation and keep unemployment down. While it's true that the Fed does not have the power of the purse, it does have the power of the pulpit. When it speaks, those in power hang on its every word. When the national debt crisis blows up, unemployment will skyrocket, and it will almost certainly bring on a recession. The Fed, at a minimum, should have been pounding the table, warning Capitol Hill of the risks associated with unbalanced budgets and the ballooning national debt. On this matter, it failed miserably.

When I wrote that paragraph, I had Ben Bernanke in mind. I don't recall Janet Yellen, the current head of the Federal Reserve, forcefully addressing this issue either.

Summing Up!

I set up an impossible goal for myself. I am a strong believer in America and the values our founders put into place through the laws that govern this country. I take pride in what American exceptionalism brings to its citizens, and, at the same time, I am frustrated by the fact that most Americans haven't a clue as to the true meaning of that phrase. I am frustrated by the actions our government is taking in limiting our ability to live our lives as we see fit, instead controlling more and more of it. I could go on and on, but I think you get my point. In any case, I feel that my unique background gives me some insight on the national debt and most of the factors associated with it. My goal in this book has been to alert our citizens about the crisis facing our country.

I have to come to terms with the fact that the national debt issue doesn't have a big following. But even more important is the fact that the resolving the national debt issue will cause great pain to America and its citizens. But if America is going to represent the world's strong values, it will only be able to do that from a position of strength. Only by addressing the national debt problem can we continue to prosper and show people across the globe what true freedom is.

About the Author

I describe myself as a portly, often-grumpy, seventy-five-year-old, retired single man. I completed two years of high school and joined the US Air Force at the age of seventeen, where I got my GED. After a few feeble attempts at jobs, I took a clerical position with a Wall Street firm. I remained on Wall Street for the rest of my working career (roughly thirty-three years). I retired unwillingly at the age of fifty-eight due to a disability.

The reason I didn't finish high school is a long story, but I confess I wasn't exactly a model student. I then chose the military option. The air force gives all new recruits an aptitude test to determine what jobs they might be best suited for. Much to my surprise, they assigned me to the intelligence division. After some schooling, I was assigned the job of reviewing Russian radio traffic to scan for relevant intelligence information.

My military experience had no value in the business world. I held a clerical position for my entire three-and-a-half years at E. F. Hutton. I was in my fifth year of a twenty-year stint at Paine Webber before I was given my first supervisory position. About five years after that, I became a methods and procedures analyst. My job was to look at the way many departments in the firm performed their functions and devise procedural changes that would cut costs. Ironically, senior management found another way to cut costs, and that was to eliminate the methods and procedures department.

A few years later, I became a credit analyst at Paine Webber and eventually became an assistant vice president and co-manager of the credit department, which was staffed by six MBAs. We were responsible for setting trading limits (credit lines) for institutional accounts that traded in Treasury and mortgage-backed securities. The company's institutional customer base consisted mostly of broker dealers, commercial banks, mortgage bankers, and savings-and-loan institutions.

Credit limits are a regulatory requirement that served to protect Paine Webber from losses in case an institutional customer walked away from its trades. Transactions in mortgage-backed securities were usually made for multiple millions of dollars and were completed on a forward basis—that is, buy now, pay later. Some of these trades took many months to settle. The firm traded billions in securities every week.

Credit limits were extended based on the financial strength of the institution. A determination was made as to how much of a loss the institutional customer could absorb without putting itself at risk. In order to determine a credit limit, we would complete a thorough review of the institution's financial statements. Needless to say, this required extensive knowledge of how these institutions functioned.

After leaving Paine Webber, I joined Nomura Securities, the US subsidiary of the giant Japanese broker. At the time, Nomura Securities was one of about thirty-five primary dealers through which the government sold newly issued Treasury securities to institutions. I managed the reporting function that the Federal Reserve required of dealers. (As of August 2015, the number of primary dealers had been whittled down to twenty-two.)

I don't know exactly how accurately the other primary dealers were in their reporting, but when I performed this function for Nomura, I found that two of the reporting requirements were in fact not doable. When Nomura challenged the Fed on this, it responded that we must be wrong because the other primary dealers did not have the same problem. After a few letters to and meetings with the Fed, we were ultimately proven correct, and the bank changed both of the reporting requirements. I think most of the other primary dealers probably knew of the problem but ignored it because they didn't want to draw the attention of the Federal Reserve. They took the "if it ain't broke, don't fix it" attitude.